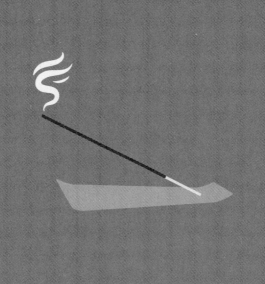

THE
BAD
VIBES
FIELD GUIDE

ABOUT THE AUTHOR

Devin Hunter is a bestselling author of *The Witch's Book of Power*, *The Witch's Book of Spirits*, *The Witch's Book of Mysteries*, the critically acclaimed *Modern Witch*, and *Crystal Magic for the Modern Witch*. Initiated into multiple occult orders, Devin is the founder of the Sacred Fires Tradition of Witchcraft and co-founder of the Black Rose Tradition of Witchcraft. He hosts the *Modern Witch* podcast, recommended by the *AV Club* and *Glamour*, and he's co-owner of Datura Trading Co. Visit him at ModernWitch.com/Devin.

THE

BAD VIBES

FIELD GUIDE

A DEFINITIVE HANDBOOK
FOR PSYCHICS
AND THE AFFLICTED

DEVIN HUNTER

FOREWORD BY **M. BELANGER**

LLEWELLYN
WOODBURY, MINNESOTA

FIRST EDITION
First Printing, 2025

Book design by Rebecca Zins
Cover design by Kevin R. Brown
Illustration on page 103 by Llewellyn Art Department

Llewellyn Publications is a registered trademark of Llewellyn Worldwide Ltd.

Library of Congress Cataloging-in-Publication Data (Pending)
ISBN: 9780738778419

Llewellyn Worldwide Ltd. does not participate in, endorse, or have any authority or
responsibility concerning private business transactions between our authors and the
public.
All mail addressed to the author is forwarded but the publisher cannot, unless specifically instructed by the author, give out an address or phone number.
Any internet references contained in this work are current at publication time,
but the publisher cannot guarantee that a specific location will continue to be maintained. Please refer to the publisher's website for links to authors' websites and other
sources.

Llewellyn Publications
A Division of Llewellyn Worldwide Ltd.
2143 Wooddale Drive
Woodbury, MN 55125-2989
www.llewellyn.com

Printed in the United States of America

FOR MOJO, WHO BROUGHT ALL THE GOOD VIBES.

CONTENTS

Exercise List...x

Foreword by M. Belanger...xiii

Introduction...1

(((**Start Here in Case of Emergency!** 7)))

PART ONE
Sensing Vibrations · 11

1: Anatomy of a Vibration   15

2: Identifying a Vibration   41

PART TWO
Bad Vibrations · 65

3: Our Bad Vibes   69

4: Other People's Bad Vibes   87

5: Environmental and Preternatural Bad Vibes   107

PART THREE
Cleansing and Triage · 127

6: Foundations of Psychic Cleansing   131

7: The Scale of Cleansing, Part One   153

8: The Scale of Cleansing, Part Two   177

PART FOUR
Protection and Transmutation · 193

9: Your Personal Security System   197

10: Transmutation and Reformatting Vibes   223

Conclusion...237

Bibliography and Recommended Reading...239

Index...245

EXERCISE LIST

1: Core Beliefs   26

2: Simple and Effective Grounding and Centering   30

3: Making Contact with the Higher Self   31

4: Focusing and Connecting to Source   34

5: Pouring and Directing Flows of Source   36

6: Lasers!   37

7: Scanning Mind, Body, and Spirit   43

8: Source Scan   44

9: Pendulum Scan   47

10: Scanning with Tarot   49

11: Meeting Your Guides, Part One   57

12: Meeting Your Guides, Part Two   58

13: Self Shadow Work   78

14: Cord Cutting   92

15: Channeling the Elements   139

16: Iron Activation   142

17: Simple Salt Cleansing Bath   145

18: Sonic Clearing   148

19: Reorientation   158

20: Source Star for Self and Immediate Surroundings   164

21: Curse Removal   165

22: Positive Imprinting   168

23: Iron Plug (Slow Method)   171

24: Creating a Ley Line Tributary (Faster Method)   172

25: Etheric Stent   174

26: Running Current   180

27: Crossing a Spirit Over   182

28: Bridge Reading   184

29: Eviction   185

30: Building the Inner Temple   203

31: The Inner Protective Layer   205

32: The Middle Intermediary Layer   207

33: The Outer Protective Layer   208

34: Getting a Recommendation from Your Guide   211

35: Creating an Intentional Thoughtform   212

36: Programming the Security Network   219

37: Shields Up!   220

38: Hydro Transmutation   225

39: Creating an Ambient Psychic Transmutation System   227

40: Elemental Transmutation   230

FOREWORD

We've all felt them—bad vibes. Coming from that one room in your house; from that otherwise normal-looking street along your walk; from that new coworker everyone's learned to avoid. There may be nothing concrete that tips you off to trouble. The "bad" room in your house is otherwise perfectly mundane. You keep it well lit. The clutter doesn't build up. Even so, at certain points in the day (or night), something's not right. You can't see anything physically different with the space, but you feel it like an itch on the wrong side of your skin: the vibe is off.

Even if you don't think of yourself as psychic, empathic, or particularly sensitive, chances are you've had at least one experience like this. An instinct, an intuition, or a bone-deep body-feel that something is wrong. And you probably didn't listen to those cues at first, but then something happened and you *know*—those feelings were there for a reason.

Bad vibes. Everyone gets them.

But what do you do about those feelings? Just avoid the room or the street or the off-putting coworker? Bad vibes are everywhere, and you can't contort your life around them, certainly not if you want to continue living in a comfortable and fulfilling way. It's easy to feel powerless, especially as our world seems to grow increasingly more chaotic and confrontational. You could ask for help, of course. There are plenty of skilled folks out there who can clear negative energy, whether they use prayers or charms or the borrowed indigenous practice of smudging. Helping clear hauntings and negative energies from peoples' homes was something I did for years both on-screen and off when working for television shows such as *Paranormal Lockdown* and *Paranormal State,* so I know. But wouldn't you rather learn how to clear up all those bad vibes on your own?

That's what this book is all about.

We all know the saying: give a person a fish and they'll eat for a day; teach them how to fish and they'll eat for a lifetime. It's the same with protection from things like bad vibes. Even though it requires more investment, the long-term solution is best. You may not always be positioned to call in an expert to help you cope. It is far better to learn what bad vibes are, what situations may cause them, and—most importantly—how to handle them on your own when you're under their effects.

Devin Hunter, the author of this guide, is one of those people who gets called up to sort out bad vibes, from hauntings to negative attachments to other instances of psychic distress. He grew up in a house with very bad vibes of its own (that's his story to tell later in the book—I won't spoil it). Devin's experiences in that home helped motivate him to learn how to protect himself as well as others, starting from a place of necessity then expanding to a place of curiosity and determination. Decades later, he's developed an arsenal of versatile techniques that he's eager to share for your own solutions.

One of the strengths about his book is Devin has been there: he's been the kid hiding under the blankets *knowing* something is wrong but lacking the frame of reference to do anything about it. With time and practice, he's learned what bad vibes are and how to deal with them, and his own haunted history has given him deep compassion for those who have no context for their experiences and are left feeling confused, frustrated, and scared.

It's totally okay to be scared, especially when you don't know how to make what you're experiencing stop. But the good news is, Devin has collected all the tools right here that you'll need to reclaim your sense of safety.

Think of the *Bad Vibes Field Guide* as a first aid book for psychic emergencies. So many people seek out books like this because they're in distress, and Devin understands that. So, he starts off with what amounts to a jump-start guide for dealing with your problem in whatever way your personal experience of bad vibes might manifest. That section is essentially psychic triage; it helps you get out of crisis before you attempt anything else. Devin understands the urgency and provides tools that are simple and effective. You don't have to worry about mastering obscure terminology or understanding complicated theories about energy work or psychic phenomenon for these methods to work. Devin provides results-oriented techniques accessible to anyone.

If you are in crisis, go there first. That section starts on page 7.

Once you have your oxygen mask on, so to speak, then it's time to dig deeper into the concept of bad vibes—what they are, why we experience them, and how we can prevent further crises going forward. There are plenty of techniques that will help you in an emergency, but the long-term focus is on preventative measures. Devin is a skillful guide, but not one who talks down to you. The language throughout this book is accessible. Each step of the way, Devin presents his theories and exercises in an easy-going, conversational tone that helps you feel seen and supported.

Even his choice of terminology for the focus of this book—*bad vibes* as opposed to "haunting" or "negative energy" or half a dozen other charged terms—is a conscious one that makes all the information gathered here feel more relatable. Devin holds careful intentionality for inclusion, mindful that everyone is coming from different backgrounds, different belief systems, and widely varying levels of confidence and expertise.

Devin is writing from a place of multidisciplinary esoteric expertise (magick, energy work, witchcraft, psychic development), all of it informing the exercises, insights, and advice collected in this manual. Everything here is valuable, but perhaps the single most inspired element of this book comes not from Devin's studies in magick but his background in music. Using the analogy of music—specifically sound waves—Devin offers an explanation of vibes and how they impact us that will instantly make sense to anyone.

I don't want to give too much of it away because I think it's important to experience the reasoning in Devin's own words, but once you learn to look at vibes (bad or otherwise) as sounds in our environment—sounds that we may experience harmoniously or discordantly—then managing our reactions to those vibes becomes easy. This sound wave model of psychic energy Devin offers is also incredibly empowering. It reframes experiences that other books might label as psychic attacks and reminds us instead that sometimes we react negatively to a vibe not because that vibe itself is inherently negative or even dangerous but simply because it doesn't mesh with us in that moment. The solution can be as simple as changing our own vibration and moving on.

Shifting the discourse away from terms such as "negative energy" and "psychic attack" while redirecting it to something as simple as *vibes* is brilliant because that old, charged language often comes heftily laden with a baggage of fear. Fear gives things power, even when they don't deserve to hold that power.

Removing the implicit sense of danger most people feel when they first experience bad vibes—or at least providing cogent reasons to remain calm—is perhaps the most useful tool in the mighty arsenal gathered here. When I did haunting resolution myself on *Paranormal State,* one of the biggest hurdles families experienced when bad vibes infringed upon their living spaces was their very understandable fear. That fear made them vulnerable to further crises, but they had no way to banish that fear until they could also understand what they were dealing with, what it was capable of doing to them, and how to make it stop.

All of that knowledge is collected right here, woven in language that anyone will be able to understand.

With Devin's guidance, get ready to take your power back. It's time.

—M. BELANGER

INTRODUCTION

Even though I have written introductions before, I am finding this particular introduction a bit hard to pin down because this is a book I have waited a long time to write. My propensity is to jump in with battle stories from being a professional psychic for twenty years, but my instinct tells me that most people picking this book up will have enough on their plate already. The world can be a dark and scary place, and chances are you have come into contact with some of that darkness. Perhaps you are even experiencing some of it now and aren't sure what to do. Alternatively, perhaps you are just a weirdo like me and are into this sort of stuff; either way, you have come to the right place.

Bad vibes are hard to quantify in a tangible sense. They aren't something we can hold or explain to others in measurable terms. However, if you say someone or something has "bad vibes," people instantly understand on a visceral level what you mean. These vibes are something the average person can sense in an instinctual manner. Sometimes, these bad vibes are small hunches, and sometimes, they are ghoulish fiends.

While discussion of such things is usually relegated to those interested in the psychic and the spiritual, we don't need to possess a spiritual gift in order to know when the energy around us is off or when we are in a situation that isn't good for us. Our instincts have developed over millions of years to alert us when something is amiss. The only comfort this can really provide us is the knowledge that we are preprogrammed to sense vibrations, but knowing that and embracing it can be a difficult road for many.

Knowing we are supposed to sense vibrations also doesn't address their cause or how to deal with them when they become part of our lives and we don't want them to. For those answers we must turn to the psychic, the spiritual, and the preternatural, stepping into the strange and unknown. Admittedly, the realm of the spiritual isn't always the best place to look, as we will discuss later in the book, but it is the most likely place where you will find answers. We needn't rely on religion for evidence; cultures around the world are filled with symbols and talismans meant to ward off bad vibes and bring in the good. Our mythologies are rife with stories that explain these things, or at least try to, and our tribal histories are loaded with examples of how our ancestors dealt with them. Psychics, mystics, and occultists have always been part of the scene that is addressing the palpable and unseen forces influencing our lives. Some of it is bullshit, sure, but most of it is useful, and that's why we keep it and integrate it into our lives even in the modern era.

HOW I CAN HELP

There are times when instinct and tradition fail us, however. That is when you call someone like me to come and take a look. I mentioned earlier that I have been a professional psychic for twenty years. The term professional psychic is an easy catchall for the odd line of work that I stumbled into and still find myself enthralled by all these years later. I also go by witch, sorcerer, and exorcist; whatever makes me more palatable for my client. I fully understand they are all equally as damning, yet each label fits me like a glove.

Specifically, my talents are in the area of mediumship (spirit communication) and psychic energy projection (energy movement), skills that are only useful in niche situations. I have developed a reputation for taking cases that most consider to be lost causes. People come to me when they've exhausted all other options and have nowhere else to turn, most come as referrals from other mediums. I'm the guy you call when someone gets pushed down a flight of stairs by invisible hands, when they've become bedridden for months with an unexplained illness, when the priest comes to bless the house but runs away (yeah, that really happened). I'm the guy who gets the frantic message to come help when the things that go bump in the night get rowdy, and I absolutely love my job, even though I wish it didn't need to exist.

At the heart of what I do is the belief that a problem can't resolve itself until the person afflicted learns how to respond to whatever is causing the affliction. I believe in a holistic approach that puts my clients and students into the driver's side, which is why I believe I get results. Often the most effective treatment is one that considers multiple angles.

Despite what most would think before getting to know me, I am a skeptical and science-minded person. I spend a lot of time trying to prove that something isn't real before I accept that it is. I have a background in psychology, and I am a big proponent of mental health. I am not a therapist; I can help you with the ghosts in your attic not the skeletons in your closet, but counseling does end up being a big part of what I do. In addition to the power of the spirit, I believe in the power of the mind and know what it is capable of when we are pushed to our limits, something I find particularly valuable when confronting the damned.

Early on in my career, I became aware that there are thousands of people just like me out there. Their unique set of gifts may vary, but there are psychics and spiritually aware individuals who want to help because they also have been personally affected by bad vibes. I have grown particularly invested in wanting to help those people develop their skill and know-how, wherever that might lead them. When there is real suffering and confusion in the world, we need as many people as possible responding on the front lines, on this plane and in the next.

HOW TO USE THIS BOOK

This book is for both the newly afflicted and the sage advisor. I wanted to write something that could be useful at any level of experience, regardless of what you are facing. In part because there is any number of potential scenarios one might find themselves facing, but also because those who encounter bad vibes big enough to take action on will often find themselves dealing with all number of spiritual matters in their lifetimes. I wanted to write something that would grow with those people as their skills and experience unfold.

To make this happen, we are going to cover a wide range of topics with varying degrees of intensity. Each topic will build upon the one that precedes it, and we are going to pause to process and develop useful skills along the way. People looking for quick answers will find step-by-step procedures to tackle their issues and those looking to explore more of the how and why of it all will find a trove of valuable tools and exercises from my own practice to help them expand their abilities.

We are going to look at how to cleanse, how to protect ourselves from, and how to transmute bad vibes, regardless of their size, construct, or origin. We will cover everything from how to find and remove psychic residue to how to deal with unwanted ghosts and how to turn spiteful energy into a nutritious supplement for the soul. We will explore a myriad of topics from the psychic output of anxiety to how to get rid of those pesky shadow-people once and for all. I have taken special care to include as much information as I possibly could about our subjects and have curated lists of other books and authors whose work can help your search should you find a topic here interesting and want to explore it further.

I'm going to say something to you now that I have always wanted to say in an introduction—book lovers, forgive me. While you read this, I encourage you to highlight the words that feel powerful; take a pencil and write notes in the margins, underline important passages, and record your thoughts; earmark the pages—do whatever you need to make this book useful. I also encourage you to have a journal. At the end of each chapter, you'll see writing prompts that are there to help you make sense of how the material can better personally apply to you or the situation at hand. When I teach classes, these are the same prompts I use with students to facilitate group discussion, so please feel free to be as chatty as you want in your responses.

In closing, I just wanted to say that I know all of this is weird and that even talking about it can be an uncomfortable experience. It is because of the awkwardness surrounding much of this that bad vibes are allowed to thrive. By taking ourselves seriously, even if we can't make sense of what we are experiencing in the moment, we take the first steps in reclaiming our power. As we will explore, that power is what all of this is really about in the end. Trust yourself and trust in your ability to face whatever it is that might be taunting you from the shadows. You got this.

START HERE
IN CASE OF EMERGENCY!

Start here if you need exercises that can make an immediate difference in a vibrational emergency situation. Keep in mind that whatever bad vibes you are battling right now want you feeling as powerless as possible in this moment. Don't let them win! As you perform these exercises, do everything you can to surround yourself with your version of positivity, whatever that might be. Follow these guidelines starting now and come back to the rest of the material when you feel ready to take on the rest of the world. For now, let's take care of what ails you.

Recite this core belief as an affirmation:

> I am safe and protected. I am worthy and loved.
> I am in control of my mind, body, and soul.
> My spirit is wise; it knows what to do. My
> vibration is strong; it overrides all others. My
> intention is clear; it takes precedent over my
> fear. I am capable. I am powerful. I am in control.

Recite this often and whenever you start to feel yourself losing nerve.

. . . .

Avoid media that makes you feel anything less than happy to be alive. Listen to stuff that makes you feel good and watch shows and movies that make you laugh, but avoid anything too serious or too emotional. We need to keep your headspace as light as possible.

• • • •

Avoid mind-altering substances. Again, headspace is important. It might not be fun, but you should avoid alcohol, marijuana, and other mind-altering substances for a few days. Being anything other than clearheaded when in spiritual crisis will only exacerbate the issue and keep you from being able to see a resolution.

• • • •

Take two showers a day, being sure to stand with the water running over your head for around ten minutes. As you do this, focus on the sensation of the water rolling over your body and visualize it removing unwanted psychic energy. The sensation is key, as it helps to relax psychic muscles that are likely stressed in addition to physically stimulating blood flow, which is good for energy flow.

• • • •

If possible, replace one of those showers with a bath containing two cups of table salt (for a full bath) and soak for at least ten minutes, rinsing off when finished in the shower. If you don't have a bathtub, you can make a quick salt scrub for the shower to be used once a day by mixing half a cup of your favorite body wash with a cup of table salt. Gently scrub your body (avoiding the face) with the mix and rinse thoroughly. Salt helps to break energetic patterns and is especially useful when one is under spiritual attack.

• • • •

Dance when you feel you can. Yeah. Really. I know it sounds ridiculous but it's good for stimulating life force, and you need as much of that as possible. Even if all you are capable of doing is wiggling your pinky toe to your favorite tune, do it.

· · · ·

Avoid sex with people you aren't deeply connected to and sex that doesn't make you happy. Junk-food sex is only going to deplete your life force, and during sex is when we are most psychically open and vulnerable.

· · · ·

Avoid people who are agents of bad vibes or who are connected to the vibes you are trying to separate from.

· · · ·

If you have access to LED color-changing lights, as are the fashion in many homes, sit in a room filled with purple light for two hours. Green and orange lights are also particularly useful in stimulating the psychic channels.

· · · ·

Light incense, preferably cleansing mixes containing frankincense or copal, but anything that you have a positive association with will work.

· · · ·

Drink tea containing lavender, lemon, ginger, or rosemary, as those herbs are known to help clear negative energy and stimulate the flow of personal energy.

(((PART ONE)))

SENSING VIBRATIONS

When I was a little boy, we lived in what was undeniably one of the most haunted houses that I have ever set foot in. My time there wasn't the beginning of my spiritual connection with the other side, but it was the beginning of my fascination with the preternatural. The whole experience could have been a Stephen King novel, and it took a long time after we moved before we could even talk about it as a family.

The house was old—parts of it were from the Civil War era—and the entire time we lived there it was under renovation, requiring constant repair. We eventually found out that it had been part of the Underground Railroad. To the best of my recollection, there were four distinct spirits that called it home. At the time of writing this, the property has been sold off to a farming corporation and the house demolished.

We spent around eight months there before breaking the lease, and during that time, I experienced things that I still find upsetting to this day. I am open about a lot of my past, but even I find it difficult to talk about what happened there because it was so unreal. I was plagued by nightmares the whole time we lived there and would wake up to a dark figure sharing my pillow. At least once a week, it would shake my bed just to mess with me.

The spirits there had an ear for old-school twangy country music and insects, both of which would show up at the strangest times. Once I was attacked by wasps in the middle of winter in my room. Then the family dog almost died after being attacked by hundreds of ticks just a few weeks later during a snowstorm. Bobo Bear, the dog and our fierce protector, was diagnosed with a rare sickness called "tick paralysis" at the emergency vet, which happens when there are so many ticks present that the neurotoxin they release builds up and actually paralyzes the body. He was well cared for and there is no way we would have missed one tick, let alone hundreds. Also, did I mention it was the middle of winter? He survived, and it took months to nurse him back to health. Unfortunately, we had to give him to another family for fear of what would happen if we brought him back to that house.

There are so many things that happened there, but what I remember most is the feeling of being helpless and trapped. I remember the fearful look on my mother's face when she didn't know what to do and my sister screaming as she ran out of her bedroom. Sometimes experiencing bad vibes is just our way of responding to someone's negative energy, but sometimes the experience is dark and complicated.

People I have told the story to ask if I would go back now if the house were still there, and my answer is always a resounding yes. I would have a very different experience today than I did back then, and I am a lot harder to mess with. It all boils down to knowing where my power is in these situations and how to identify unwanted energies more effectively, which happen to be the focus of the next two chapters.

WHAT YOU'LL FIND

Before we can face whatever might be at the root of the bad vibes that enter our life, we have to figure out what exactly we are dealing with and what exactly we can do about it. We also need to prepare ourselves for the occasion so we can confidently enter that experience without fear.

Part 1 is a crash course into what makes a vibration something we can sense and ways that we can use our spiritual and psychic gifts to interact with them directly. We cover a lot of ground, with my ultimate goal being to prepare you for investigating the bad vibrations that you encounter.

I will mention certain practices that might be a bit too much for some, which is why I do my best to offer options wherever I can. I also try to present these topics to you without the lens of any one religion. Feel free to make this your own and to include your personal religious techniques or views wherever it is appropriate. Try to keep an open mind when possible. My hope is always to make all this easier for you, not scarier or more complicated.

1

ANATOMY OF A VIBRATION

Something we will discuss throughout this entire book is the concept that you, as a psychic and spiritual being, can use your skills to bring life into harmony. Unfortunately, it isn't always easy, and I think being psychically sensitive makes it more difficult at times than it ought to be. That said, the goal of seeking out and understanding energetic harmony is quintessential to understanding when something is off, how it is off, and what it will take to fix it.

In this chapter, I am going to make the case that you have spiritual and psychic energy even if you don't consider yourself to be a particularly psychic or spiritual person. I am going to be honest and discuss how being psychically sensitive can kind of suck sometimes and how bad vibes can take advantage of that, but I'm also going to share with you what I do to take my power back.

For those who are new to all this, the skills we dive into here will translate into a show of spiritual force when confronting bad vibrations in later chapters. Those experienced with their receptive spiritual gifts will also find tools for turning those abilities into projective skills. Believe it or not, being psychic doesn't necessarily mean always being on the receiving end of energy—we can direct psychic energies in our life as well.

I have a music background, and over the years I have grown to include music theory and music production as a means of explaining what goes on in the psychic world. I find that it's easier to think of psychic energy in terms of sound waves. Even if you are hearing-impaired, the science behind sound waves and harmony is still a solid metaphor for what we experience.

VIBRATIONS

Vibrations—those things that are hard to pin down in words—are called *vibrations* for a reason. Like sound, they emanate from a source and travel through space until they either dissipate or come in contact with a receiver. Sound is energy traveling through space, and we can feel the force of that vibration as a physical sensation when we are in the area of its effect.

Similarly, when those who aren't embracing their psychic abilities and working with them interact with a vibe, good or bad, it's experienced through physical sensation. Symptoms include anything from a headache and nausea to euphoria and bliss, depending on what the source is and how its vibration is affecting the environment and/or the receiver.

We have a vibration as well, which is the most important piece of the puzzle. When our vibration comes in contact with other vibrations, one or two different things happen: they meet harmonically or have dissonance. When they are harmonic, they produce a shared vibration that, generally, feels positive in nature. We sense them as enjoyable and inviting, even cozy. However, when there is dissonance, the two vibrations are at odds with one another. This doesn't make either bad. The sensation of dissonance often feels disagreeable, but it just means that they aren't complimentary to one another, and the effect is experienced as a negative one. Energetic harmony produces a sense of "good vibes" whereas energetic dissonance is responsible for what are often referred to as "bad vibes."

PSYCHIC ABILITIES

I have been fortunate in my career to help people face the things that go bump in the night. I've worked on small cases where the fix was simple, and I have worked cases that haunt my dreams years after I encounter them. The golden thread that connects all of them is that my clients, regardless of the severity of their position, believed they were powerless in their situation. That's why they ultimately reached out to someone like me for help, and likely why you picked up a copy of this book.

Before we can dive into finding a fix for what ails you, we need to have what some find as an uncomfortable conversation. Hell, it is even a little awkward for me because the very topic can produce bad vibes for some.

You *are* psychic. Maybe not in the way I am, maybe not in the way the people in movies or on television are, but you are psychic. In truth, we are all psychic. It comes with the territory of being human; it's just that most of us look the other way instead of looking deeper. Being psychic is nothing more than possessing an instinctual awareness of the spiritual and psychic energies at play around you. Rarely does it look like having visions, seeing spirits, or having full conversations with the dead. For the vast majority of people, being psychic looks more like daydreaming, dissociating, and a primal compulsion to avoid certain places or people. Being psychic is so normal and everyday that most people don't consider their experiences as anything more than a personality trait and never feel the need to dive deeper.

On occasion, however, there are those of us who possess a greater propensity for sensing spiritual and psychic vibrations. We are usually what society calls psychics, mystics, shamans, witches, and so forth.

Sometimes respected, sometimes feared, we are permanent bridges between the physical and the spiritual. Some of us are born with this extra psychic sensitivity, some of us develop it at puberty or menopause, others as a result of a near-death experience.

Being psychically sensitive doesn't cue you into any hidden knowledge or enlightenment on its own. It just means we are capable of perceiving spiritual nuance, but that nuance doesn't come with a decoder ring. The most difficult element of all of this is learning how your unique set of psychic abilities work and to what degree. I will only be able to discuss the elements of psychic and spiritual development that are directly related to our work here, but I highly recommend you make a study of your psychic skills, regardless of their vigor. This will not only go a long way in helping you develop your abilities but will also help you ensure that they aren't going rogue and causing problems. I have included a list of amazing titles from fellow authors in the bibliography and recommended reading section that specifically focus on exploring your psychic abilities in depth. Check those out for inspiration; you won't regret it.

BASIC FRAMEWORK

Because the spiritual and the psychic tend to be nuanced, and we all have different backgrounds, let's go over a few basic principles that will help provide a framework for the work we will be doing together. These are points I go over with clients that help us all get on the same page and can be easily adjusted to fit into almost any worldview.

1. In the context of the spiritual, paranormal, and preternatural, the term *energy* refers to the psychic force observed interacting between objects, people, animals, and their environment. This force cannot be

measured with current technology; however, there is so much evidence to support its existence that it is only a matter of time. For now, we borrow from scientific and philosophical terminologies to help us explain the phenomenon that we witness.

2. Energy follows the path of least resistance.

3. Energy accumulates over time. This works much like gravity forming a planet. Once a sufficient amount of bad energy has been gathered in one place, it attracts other similar vibrations until it is large enough and capable of producing its own field of influence.

4. All people have psychic ability and are affected by the psychic and spiritual vibrations found both inside themselves and in their environments. Those who possess a proclivity for psychic and spiritual awareness are referred to as psychic sensitives.

5. *Life force*, *chi*, and *vital energy* are all terms used to describe aspects of personal psychic energy. All living things produce this energy, and it is among the most precious commodities in the spiritual world. In the physical world, that energy is part of a cycle of life and death, being consumed when a predator eats its prey or is redistributed when it dies and returns to the earth.

6. Life force comprises what we refer to as our "energy body" or "etheric body." This complex system is responsible for the maintenance, restoration, and overall security of the body it relates to. This energy is capable

of being projected through acts of willpower and great emotion.

7. Psychic and spiritual energy can collect over time and once a sufficient amount (or the right kind) has been collected, that energy can develop a form of consciousness. We often refer to these consciousnesses as *demons, ghosts, ghouls,* and *parasites.*

8. The planet produces its own forms of life force and has a natural filtration system for the psychic energy that it produces. This system includes ley lines, waterways, and tectonic plate boundaries. Sometimes, energy is unable to move properly in this system, causing much of the preternatural phenomenon that we encounter.

9. Our world intersects with others through the spiritual, the mental, and the psychic. Places where energy does not move normally are especially vulnerable to weaknesses in the natural boundaries between these worlds. We often refer to these places as haunted, cursed, or even as being portals between the spiritual and the material.

HOW VIBRATION AFFECTS YOU

Have you ever walked the streets of a city and taken in all the sounds? There is construction, traffic, millions of pedestrians all on their way to and fro, and some guy on a corner selling hot dogs. Imagine each of those sounds as psychic energy that is being transmitted by each of those people, what I refer to as a *frequency.*

For most people (the ones who don't acknowledge their psychic abilities or work with them), those frequencies are so omnipresent that they are easily tuned out as background noise. For the extra psychically sensitive, however, each of those frequencies are bouncing around and interacting with one another, sometimes harmonically and sometimes not. When we take a stroll through that city, we are constantly bumping into not only those frequencies, which are each capable of producing their own effect on us, but also the harmony and dissonance produced by their shared interactions.

If you live in an area where there are a lot of frequencies and interacting vibrations, learning to protect yourself and build your psychic defenses is a must. The same can be said for those who work in the psychic field helping others, those who come in contact with spirits on a regular basis, and those whose psychic abilities are becoming active, regardless of age. Cleansing, something we will talk ad nauseam about in the second part of this book, can only remain truly effective when our spiritual immune systems are boosted. Some of us build it up over time, but many, myself included, have had to make a practice out of psychic self-care in order to remain happy and healthy.

The hard part with all of this is that the bad vibes could be coming from anywhere and could have already come in contact with, and effected, other elements in our lives. Navigating our way through the metaphorical city of weird vibes (aka our lives) can be challenging for even the most prepared, so do give yourself and others some slack.

Since everything produces a vibration, we have to be aware of how those vibrations effect the people, places, and things they come in contact with. Imagine being in a crowded bar with hundreds of people all mingling and celebrating. When you first enter, the collective vibration of the space (its frequency) is overwhelming and so powerful that the initial feeling is usually one that is akin to being suppressed. The original vibration is greater than your own. After you adjust and find your people, something that allows you to integrate into the environment, that energy levels out and you become part of the larger frequency. You are now one of the hundreds participating in the overall feeling, tone, and frequency of the bar.

By simply finding your place and accepting the environment, you take on the properties of that environment and then add to its distinctiveness. As a result, you are changed and your vibration shifts. When you leave, you take a piece of that with you and, if the vibration from the bar was strong enough, you'll carry it with you until something else comes along and makes you shift your vibration. This can happen intentionally or unintentionally, and at times may be difficult, but it is something that happens quite naturally. We are social and environmental creatures, and this is just how we respond to our surroundings. We respond similarly to good and bad vibes, the only difference between the two being that good vibes are more easily accepted than those we initially feel are bad.

For those of us who accept and encourage our psychic abilities, these shifts are usually palpable, but we may not always be aware that they are taking place, or even of what to look for. With a world full of vibrations and subtle shifts, discernment of the spiritual kind can be difficult for even the most seasoned of psychics. So, what should we be looking for? Well, there are three primary symptoms that I look for.

A SHIFT IN PERSONAL PHYSICAL ENERGY

A big key that something is happening lies in the amount of personal energy we have throughout the day. What is positive or negative in the moment is subjective. However, bad vibes often have the effect of making us feel drained of personal energy while positive vibes do the opposite. Energy drains are the number one indicator that something is wrong.

Likewise, unexplained illnesses or unusual ailments, long-lasting illness, loss of sleep, lack of sexual desire, and physical depression can all be signs of the effects from a bad vibration shift.

A SHIFT IN PERSONAL FOCUS OR INTEREST

When we pick up vibes, our mind processes their energy and uses it to help construct our current version of reality. As you might imagine, good vibes make us feel like we are in the right place at the right time, like what we are focused on is bringing attention to the right things. When those vibes are bad, we are drawn further away in our thoughts from what is important to us personally, and the result is feeling a lack of focus or even like we are lost. Mental fogginess or fatigue, or an inability to be present in the moment, can be signs of a bad-vibe shift.

Circular or repetitive thoughts, addiction, and unusual or extreme sexual fantasies can all be attributed to an unwanted personal shift. Unexplained emotional shifts, malice, and suicidal thoughts are also symptoms. If you have an urge to harm yourself or others, seek immediate attention from a certified professional.

OVERSHADOWING AND ASPECTING

Overshadowing is a term I picked up from Robert Bruce, a prolific psychic development author, to describe what happens when a bad vibration is so powerful that it forces us to shift and take on attributes that overshadow our own. This is predominantly ascribed to spirit attachments, wherein we take on personality traits from the spirit or the entity, but these traits can also be environmental and not linked directly to a spirit but a location or an object. Overshadowing is generally considered a bad thing and a potential sign of light involuntary possession.

Aspecting, on the other hand, is a term first applied by occultist and psychic author Ivo Dominguez Jr. It is something we agree to happening or even welcome happening. For those who work with high-level or beneficial spirits, aspecting can help bring balance and strength to our lives. Unlike overshadowing, aspecting is consented to and permission is granted freely by the effected.

When we get to really break into the paranormal side of bad vibes, we will revisit this concept and a few more, but I want to stress the importance of identifying overshadowing as a direct sign that something paranormal is happening.

WHAT DO BAD VIBES WANT?

The specifics of what bad vibes want are situational, but the end game is always to take your power away. That is admittedly an oversimplification, but one that is not far off the mark. We will go over ways to flush out the details surrounding the different types of bad vibes as we explore the topics in this book, but it all boils down to a struggle of wills. This is especially true of conscious forms of bad vibes, such as spirit attachments. For the most part, the primary aim of bad vibes is to force us (and our vibration) into submission. This may not be a direct goal, but we can almost always distill the affects down to a struggle for vibrational superiority.

I know that sounds bleak, right? Well, it can be, which is why I said being a psychic sensitive could be a pain in the ass. There are a lot of people who get stuck on the struggle, and we are not all cut out to be spiritual warriors. Some of us just want to sleep through the night or make it through the workday without being on the receiving end of some weird vibration. The good news is that you are entirely equipped to handle anything that comes your way!

CLAIMING YOUR DIVINE AUTHORITY

While it is natural to assume that being psychic is all about being on the receiving end of spiritual vibration, that couldn't be further from reality. Our abilities work both ways. We know this because there are countless examples of this happening. Anyone who follows the Law of Attraction is using their psychic energy to manifest something they want outside of themselves. While the Law of Attraction is a shallow dip in a much larger esoteric pool, it provides just enough to help even those who don't consider themselves psychic to engage with the psychic and spiritual world.

Another example of what I call *projective psychic ability*, is in the practices of spiritual healing, including reiki. The concept that the healer is using energy they are channeling to knit the physical body back into shape clearly demonstrates the potential of training ourselves to project energy with intention.

In hopes of saving us both a lot of time, I am going to skip to the good part where I tell you how to actually flip the switch from being receptive to projective. The simple answer is that you must claim your spiritual authority. In reality, this takes a long time to truly sink in and develop; it's something that matures over a lifetime and even the best psychics in the world still consider themselves to be continual students of this process.

In order to take control over any situation (vibrational or otherwise), you must have authority to do so. In the world of the psychic and the spiritual, that authority can come from a lot of places, but most importantly it has to be discovered in you first. It is a defiant act against those energies that would otherwise diminish us or those we care for.

EXERCISE ONE
Core Beliefs

At the center of my practice to invigorate and nurture my sense of spiritual authority as a psychic, I use a lot of affirmations and positive self-talk. These techniques help us hack that relationship between the mind and the body so we can use it as a mode for psychic development. The idea is to get ourselves in the right headspace so we can engage the spiritual/psychic from a place of authority.

In my practice, I recite a core belief set (which is usually three to five phrases) at least three times before I jump into the business of approaching the energy. The following are examples of my top core belief sets, which we will be using as a jumping-off point.

CORE BELIEF SET ONE

I am safe and protected. I am worthy and loved.
I am in control of my mind, body, and soul.
My spirit is wise; it knows what to do.
My vibration is strong; it overrides all others.
My intention is clear; it takes precedent over my fear. I am capable. I am powerful. I am in control.

CORE BELIEF SET TWO

My mind, body, and soul move as one being.
What I think and feel become physical
through my being. My being gives me power
in all worlds, gives me authority over all
unwelcome vibrations, and is undeniable.

CORE BELIEF SET THREE

I am stronger than fear. Fear is a weapon
my enemy uses to intimidate and take
my power. I will not give my enemy this
weapon. I will not concede to fear.

HOW TO USE CORE BELIEF SETS

Now, listen: even if these are just personal pep talks, saying each set out loud can be a real game changer in helping us switch perspective. They allow us to carve out a pathway for our intentional energy to follow and put necessary barriers around negative thoughts that are likely being spurred by the bad vibes you are wanting to tackle. Sometimes I find myself saying them to help reconvince myself that I am, in fact, the one in control. Other times I say them as if they are a battle cry. Our main goal here is to reprogram our internal dialogue so that it is supportive of our connection to our higher selves and our spiritual support system.

YOUR HIGHER SELF

The part of you that exists beyond the physical—the spark of the Divine known in some circles as the Holy Guardian Angel, or more simply, the Higher Self—is perhaps one of the greatest mysteries we will ever encounter. It can be a little difficult to chew on at first, but I like to think of it as the piece of god(dess) inside of each of us. It is the soul between lives, the record keeper of our omni histories, and the animating force within the physical body. It is the source of our being and, in the grand scheme of things, the real us.

In many ways it is also not like us at all. If it were an actor, we would be the character they portrayed in this lifetime. For the character to meet the actor, the laws of reality must be broken. This is, essentially, what we refer to as enlightenment; when we shatter reality and meet the being behind the curtain.

What makes the Higher Self particularly powerful as an ally in protection work is that it is the purest form of Divine energy we can come into direct contact with and survive. Don't get me wrong, this is incredibly hard to do, and it takes years of practice to obtain enlightenment. We don't need to reach nirvana to contact our Higher Self. We need only to call them up and put in a request. The more time you spend learning from your Higher Self, the stronger you will grow not only as a psychic but also as a person, eventually one day reaching that elusive thing called enlightenment. What we will be doing is more akin to meeting them over video chat than meeting them in person.

CALLING THE HIGHER SELF

Let's get one thing really clear: Bad vibes hate when you are in contact with your Higher Self, and they will do anything they can to keep you from making contact, especially if you've never done it before. Remember, bad vibes feed off your unaligned state and any extra energy you can exhaust over them; it is simply in their best interest to keep you distracted, tired, and stubborn.

The reason enlightenment takes so long is because there is a whole lot of stuff between us and our Higher Selves, and bad vibes like to keep it that way. When you start to reach out for your Higher Self, don't be surprised if unexpected things try to get in your way or if there are people in your life who you start to feel no longer resonate with you. I always tell people to pay attention to what happens in their lives once they start this process, to check in with their guides often, and that it is okay to let go of behavior or people if that is a message you feel you are receiving.

To begin the process, we need to ground and center ourselves. This is critical as, like I said earlier, the Higher Self is made of some powerful stuff, and it can come on a little strong. Being able to ground energy out of your body when you are plugged into it is important not only for your spiritual and mental health but your physical body as well. In addition to burnout, you run the risk of potentially putting additional stress on the body, and that can be bad for obvious reasons. The practice of grounding and centering is also going to come up a lot as you read along, I highly recommend you run through the following exercises as I have written them at least once.

EXERCISE TWO
Simple and Effective Grounding and Centering

There are a million and one ways to do this, so let me show you my favorite easy go-to. Close your eyes and breathe slow and deep, taking each breath as fully as you naturally can. Focus on your breath for a moment and observe how air enters your nostrils or mouth, making its way to your lungs and then back out again.

Follow three or four cycles and then bring your attention to the points of stillness and silence at the beginning and the end of each breath. Pour your consciousness into those moments in between and allow yourself to sink comfortably into the present moment.

As you continue to breathe, visualize any overabundance of internal energy, be it thoughts, fear, anxiety, tension, or similar collecting inside those moments with you. Then with each exhale, purge them from your system. Once they leave your body, visualize them vaporizing, unable to continue on without you in their current form. These things are not you or your state of being, they are temporary and require your permission to exist.

Later we will learn how to transmute this energy into something we can use, but for now just focus on letting it go and taking back your permission, especially if that permission was given subconsciously. Remember, this isn't about what is happening outside of you, only what it is happening inside.

The *centering* part of the exercise refers to the mental shift that happens as a result of grounding and is the final portent that we have indeed become grounded. The hallmarks of being centered involved being clearheaded, present-minded, and less encumbered by external stress.

EXERCISE THREE
Making Contact with the Higher Self

The Higher Self is part of us, so getting in touch with it is not actually all that complicated. Having a conversation with it, on the other hand, is an entirely different book altogether. I want to caution you that like most things psychic, the results will be subtle and will likely require a greater understanding of your spiritual existence before they become anything earth-shattering. That's okay, though. We want subtle, especially in the beginning.

We want to reach up to our Higher Self because it is the seat of our divine authority and the gateway to the other worlds that intersect with our own. This exercise is designed to help you tune in to your Higher Self and draw from its influence. You may feel something physical; I usually feel a little lightheaded at first, but you also might not feel anything at all. The proof of successful contact will be in an elevated state of personal psychic energy. For me, this feels like when the coffee kicks in after breakfast, others report feeling buzzy or inspired.

It is common to receive messages during contact with the Higher Self and to have bubbles of emotional energy spring up. My recommendation is to spend some time in this state of being each day for a few minutes over the course of a week or two. This way you can (essentially) burp your energy body before you need it to do any heavy lifting.

Begin by grounding and centering yourself. Breathing in through your nose and out through your mouth, take a series of three deep breaths. As you inhale, sense the subtle energy entering your body and reserve it as you exhale. Think of it like you are taking in life force with each breath but only exhaling the air you took in when you release that breath. I visualize an iridescent white sphere of glowing energy amassing at the center of my chest.

Allow this energy to pool and gather over each breath. On the third and final exhale, tip your head backward and release all the energy you've collected upward and vocalize a *Ha* sound.

Visualize it traveling upward two or three feet in the air and hovering like a satellite. Continue to breathe with intention and allow the ball of energy to grow to a comfortable size until you feel energy start to naturally ground itself. It will feel like a calming or a settling down of the energy and may take a few minutes. My advice is to not rush this and to use your intuition for when to move on to the next step.

Once the energy begins to ground, the sphere is as large as it is going to get at the time. Focus on the sphere, which is now your personal hi-fi adapter, a piece of spiritual technology capable of helping you connect and channel the energy of the Higher Self. Conclude by reciting the fourth set of core beliefs.

CORE BELIEF SET FOUR

I am unquestionably divine, and my divinity gives me authority in this world and in others.

CHANNELING SOURCE ENERGY

Now that you've claimed your spiritual authority, you've unlocked a very important side quest that will open a whole new skill tree. By establishing those core beliefs, you have leveled up, and in doing so have reached a place where psychic abilities can intentionally shift from being receptive to being projective. By installing those core beliefs, you've installed the program that will eventually teach you how to write your own code. For now, let's focus on flipping the switch by developing a skill for channeling.

The next step as we claim our power is to learn how to channel it. This is a skill that will come in handy all throughout the book and learning to channel is a fantastic way to reinforce your connection to divinity and your spiritual authority.

Channeling is a woo-woo term for using our psychic abilities to direct flows of spiritual energy through ourselves. We not only open a channel to energy that we funnel through our spiritual body but we also direct the flow by carving a path for it to channel. This entire process is very mental and relies on our individual consciousness to take effect; however, many have been known to channel unconsciously, as an instinctual response to stress or related stimuli. When that energy is attached to a consciousness, it is possible to channel that consciousness through the spiritual body, as well. This is essentially what is happening underneath the experience of aspecting, overshadowing, and possession. I only mention this to provide context.

Channeling doesn't necessarily make one a potential target for malicious energy. If anything, those who can channel and have developed that skill proficiently are usually avoided by such beings. It is much harder to establish a connection to us, and they perceive us as dangerous, more or less because we can call in the big guns. I've listed a few books that can dive deeper into channeling than I have the ability to do here, though we will revisit the topic. As for what we need to be focused on in the moment, the next steps are simple. In fact, they are so simple most people get confused.

The trick to channeling, especially in the initial stages, is to understand that your spiritual energy is abundant and flowing on its own, with or without your help. You channel a tiny part of it every time you focus on something. When you are mentally in a place of balance and focus, you can intentionally use your thoughts as a tool for directing the flow of psychic energy. The imagination, that thing we are told to push out of the way as an adult, is the place in our minds that we will work from to do this.

What trips people up is that they expect to physically sense energy move. While that should be a goal, it isn't necessarily something everyone will experience. We don't all experience spiritual energy the same. My best advice is always to follow your gut, to listen to your intuition, and to work with your spiritual support team (spirit guides/teachers, spiritual saviors, and so on) to receive personal instruction. If you don't know your spiritual support team, hang tight, I will show you how to meet with them in a little bit. Go into channeling with Core Belief Set Three firmly in your mind, and remember that what you think and feel become physical through your being.

EXERCISE FOUR
Focusing and Connecting to Source

Our mind is a really big place, and before we can use it as a staging ground for the psychic and the spiritual, we have to learn how to navigate it. The mental landscape is a lot like the sky. Sometimes it is bright and blue, sometimes it is dark and dreary, and in just the right moments, it is clear and full of stars. Our thoughts are the things that occupy it, such as the clouds and the birds, maybe a kite or a plane, but they are not the sky. The sky, like our mind, contains many elements but cannot be described by any one of them alone.

For this exercise, I want you to begin by visualizing the mental landscape as an open sky full of things that occupy it. At first, I want you to take a moment to survey how the landscape fills itself in before we change it. Make a note in your journal about what you see there, and be sure to write down any specifics that do present themselves with clarity.

To start the process of focusing in on the specific frequency we are looking for, visualize the sky the way it would look if your mental landscape were reflective of you feeling safe, in the right place at the right time, and like you are part of something bigger than yourself. For our purposes here and wherever else this might be mentioned, we will refer to this as the "blue sky."

Somewhere in that sky is the energy we seek. This empathic trick will help you figure out where.

We can bring focus to any part of our being, but for this exercise we are going to focus on our connection to the spiritual. Think back on a memory when you knew you were spiritually connected. Think over this until you stumble upon the emotional memory from that moment. By this, I mean to try and put yourself in the emotional head space you were in at that time. Take a minute to feel this emotion, whatever that might be, sometimes it is hard to put into words, and then think of other memories that also felt like that. Over the next few minutes, surf through your thoughts as you follow this emotion throughout your life.

Now, trusting that this emotion has the right coordinates, allow it to guide you to a place somewhere inside that blue sky where your spiritual connection resides.

This is different for each of us. Depending on your religious views, your Source might take on particular attributes. For me, this place inside feels like home, like I've dialed into the part of me that is connected to my version of the ultimate spiritual being and it fills your entire field of vision. It should be like adjusting a lens to sharpen the focus.

Once you find it, look around and remember how easy it was to get there. From now on, we will refer to this as "connecting to Source."

EXERCISE FIVE
Pouring and Directing Flows of Source

This exercise builds off of the last one and allows for us to actively draw upon Source as an energy substance that can be projected.

Part One: Perform the focusing exercise. At the end, sink your consciousness back in your body while still holding on to your connection to Source. Your Source is as vast as an ocean of liquid light. Using your connection like an aqueduct, allow energy from this Source to spill over. Visualize liquid light from above traveling into the solar plexus. There, it forks into two canals, bringing this energy to both hands, where is flows freely out into your surroundings.

Part Two: Visualize the opening where you connect to Source dilating open to compensate for more energy flow. Feel this sensation and simply let it flow through you. To finish, visualize the connection slowly closing, allowing the flow of energy to naturally taper off. When finished, it might be helpful to ground if you feel excited.

EXERCISE SIX
Lasers!

To use this energy, we need to assign it a purpose. At the present moment, it is simply being funneled through you with no aim in sight. This doesn't harm you in any way, it just isn't necessarily useful for clearing.

Part One: Perform part one of the previous exercise. At this point, we can assign it almost any purpose, such as to heal or to protect, but for the intent of this exercise, we are going to direct it to clear unwanted energy. Do this by sending the mental command to this energy to cleanse any negative vibration that it comes across. In response, visualize the current of liquid light energy moving from your solar plexus to your hands, increasing in intensity and stabilizing so that what emits from your palms is now focused and laser-like.

Part Two: Visualize the opening where you connect to Source above dilating open to compensate for more energy flow. Take a few minutes to feel how this increases the energy moving through your solar plexus and hands. Finish by visualizing the connection slowly closing, allowing the flow of energy to naturally taper off. When finished, it might be helpful to ground if you feel excited.

· · · ·

Each of these exercises is going to be useful when confronting bad vibes. Practice these techniques as often as you can. Try channeling the energy into everyday items to cleanse them, as described in part one. Channel it into your bed to clear it of energy and see if you sleep better.

Channel it into your jewelry to clear it of all unwanted vibes. The more you play with this, the more potent you will be when you need these skills.

CONCLUSION AND JOURNALING

This chapter was all about getting you set up to dive into some of the stranger elements of the spiritual and psychic. We reviewed foundational exercises so that you could start to use your projective psychic muscles, and we laid the ground rules for how energy, vibration, and frequencies interact with each of us. Spend some time familiarizing yourself with the exercises and principles in this chapter before hopping over to the next chapter.

Before we move on, take a few minutes to respond to the following journal prompts so we can take what we learned here even further.

1. How does it feel when you are grounded and centered versus when you are ungrounded? If you could take a before and after shot of your mind, what would they look like?

2. What does Source energy feel like to you? Is there an accompanying sensation, physical or otherwise?

3. When you performed the focusing and connecting to Source exercise and visualized your mental landscape as the sky, how did it initially appear to you? What were the things occupying it? What do you think those individual elements represent, if anything?

4. How do you feel after you have channeled Source energy? Are there any residual sensations?

5. We discussed spirit guides at length in this chapter. What are your experiences before doing the exercises related to spirit guides, if any? How do your previous experiences compare to your experiences while performing the exercises in this chapter?

6. We went over four core beliefs that will help you when facing bad vibes. Create one more core belief to add to the set based on your goals as a spiritual agent.

2
IDENTIFYING A VIBRATION

In the previous chapter, we looked at how vibrations work and manifest and discussed what bad vibrations ultimately want from us. We will continue to hash out these concepts as we move along, but for now, we need to get a wee bit more prepared before we begin to engage the bad vibes around us. In this chapter, we are going to take a look at how I both prepare for dealing with vibes and what I do to get the answers about the bad vibes I am facing, when I need them.

Those who are less experienced with the psychic and spiritual will find a chapter full of exercises and techniques that will become invaluable in their practice over time, like working with spirit guides to get important information or scanning the energy within a certain place. Readers who are more experienced will find a simplified and practical approach to communing with their environment that can make investigations a breeze, even when a medium isn't present.

SCANNING AND SENSING VIBES

I'm not a big fan of terms like *positive* or *negative* energy because they make life seem a lot more adversarial than it really is. What is positive or negative, just like what is good or bad, is subjective. It depends on the factors and the situation, and when it comes to the psychic and the spiritual, there is always nuance. What matters isn't necessarily if something is positive or negative in a moral sense, though there will be times where that will be an issue for some, but rather if the vibration and frequency are harmonious and in resonance or if they are dissonant and inharmonious. When scanning for vibrations, the number one rule is to not get caught up in all the trappings, but to first be an observer.

To circle back to music theory for a moment, chords are when three or more notes (vibrations) are played in unison and the result is harmony. Minor chords are major or "pleasant sounding" chords that are altered by dropping the pitch (frequency) of one of the notes. The result is usually something that sounds haunting or not complete but still contains harmony. In most music, minor chords are resolved by playing the major chord. In short, dissonance isn't always a bad thing and might even lead to something beautiful. Nuance is everything!

Scanning for a vibe is a very simple thing to do on paper; however, in practice it can be more challenging than we would expect. I prefer to bounce between three methods to help me discern information when necessary. I use these methods to check my work when I need a second opinion. The first is a Source scan, which involves actively engaging your psychic senses to perform the scan. The second is dowsing, which is an ancient practice that emerged within different cultures throughout the world, specifically in our case with a pendulum. The last being the tarot, which is particularly good at providing nuance and detail. Try all three and keep the practice that works best for you.

For me the challenge isn't doing the scan or acting on it, more so that there are days when I don't feel especially plugged in because of allergies or the side effects of allergy medication, so dowsing and tarot help break through whatever fog might be there. Both dowsing and tarot can be faster than our unaided psychic senses in many cases. They are tools for our psychic abilities and can make life so much easier. You don't need to work with all of these methods, or even one of them, but you do need to have a tool kit at your disposal. I am perfectly okay with you borrowing mine. For those who are into paranormal investigating, developing these methods can assist you when a sensitive psychic or a medium cannot be present.

For this chapter, I am going to introduce each method as we scan for harmony and dissonance in your life. Think of this purely as a fact-finding mission meant to engage your psychic senses. What you do with that information is up to you. Should you want to investigate it further, the exercises in this book can help you find more answers.

EXERCISE SEVEN
Scanning Mind, Body, and Spirit

One of my favorite practices involves checking in with the mind, body, and spirit and making sure that they are in harmony. It has been around in some form or another since antiquity, and while it has gone by many names and has been presented in many ways, its value is undeniable and it always leads to mindfulness. If we can identify what harmony looks and feels like inside ourselves, we are one step closer to discerning that in others.

Find a few minutes to check in with yourself and simply observe your current state of being. Think about your physical condition, observe the thoughts that arise as you do, and let them go. Think about your mental condition and do the same. Finally, lift your thoughts to your spiritual condition and do the same.

EXERCISE EIGHT
Source Scan

Source scanning is a term I coined for the process of using our psychic senses to touch base with a person, a place, or a thing and observing. We are using our psychic abilities to scan for present frequencies or vibrations and then tracing them back to their source. We are going to expand upon this process over the next few chapters. More elaborate variations will require us to do a bit more prep work, but for now all you need is a (preferably quiet) place free from distraction where you can close your eyes and think in peace for a few moments.

Bring your attention back to your breath and the present moment. Once you feel ready, bring your attention to your body and slowly check in with it as you bring your focus upward from your toes to the top of your head. Don't rush this; use it as an opportunity to honor your body and to warm up your psychic senses. How does your body feel? Where is there tension, pain, or discomfort, if any? If you have none, you surely must still be in your early twenties or teens and have yet to experience the pleasures of aging, but for the rest of us, once you identify that discomfort, bring your awareness to it.

Much of what we do as psychics, beyond the sensing, is to follow a vibe as a dog might follow a scent. The discomfort is a symptom, and our job is to trace the symptom back to its cause (i.e., its source). Identify if the discomfort is producing other symptoms, for example, when you bring your attention to a pain in your back, are you suddenly aware of a general feeling of depression, or of other aches? Once you have a greater view of the symptoms and how they might be interconnected, ask your body why it feels this way.

Let your body talk to you and remember that it isn't going to communicate with words, it is going to communicate as impulses, as pictures, and through symbols, so be prepared for anything. Don't try to interpret the information at first, just let your body respond; our job for the time being is to only observe. Our bodies are made of the earth, they connect us to physicality and material being, that comes with a lot of discomfort throughout our lives. Once you have the information, take a moment to write it down and then bring yourself back to focusing on your breath.

When you're ready, take a moment to follow your breath and then bring your attention to your mind. Your mind, which is this complicated thing, can be hard to conceptualize. Instead of thinking about an empty room or building, think of it like the sky. Particularly, the view of the sky when you are laying on your back and looking up. Your mind is as vast and endless as the sky from this vantage point, and your thoughts are the clouds and the airplanes that move through it. They aren't your mind, just things that occupy its space.

Take a few moments to identify the largest clouds and bring your attention to them. Just like when we asked our body to show us why it felt a certain way, we are going to ask our minds why these clouds are so large. Why do they take up so much space? This response will come easier than that of the first. Don't argue with yourself, just observe and record the information in your journal.

Finally, bring your attention back to your breath. When you're ready, return to the sky of the mind and continue to breathe slow and deep. Bring your attention not to the clouds or the planes but the blue emptiness between them. Follow your gaze outward into the sky, through the things that occupy it, and beyond into a place of emptiness and stars. Suspended at the center of the solar system is the sun, a representation of that divine spark inside of you. Around it are planets, asteroid belts, moons and other satellites, each representative of your greater spiritual knowledge, purpose, and history.

Your inner solar system is as unique as you are. Spend a few moments looking around at what fills the space therein. When you are ready, find one of those galactic bodies that most draws your attention and turn your attention to it, moving through space until you can get a better view. Ask it as you have asked other aspects of yourself before, why am I drawn to you? What do you represent? Observe. Let it speak to you in its own language, which could be through anything from a memory to sudden inspiration. When you are ready, return to your version of Earth's sky, that place of your mind, and open your eyes. Record whatever information you found.

The mind-body-spirit (MBS) system is complex, and as you can tell, there is a lot that we can learn by exploring each of them and even their connection to one another. We will do this as much as possible where relevant in this text; however, I highly encourage you to learn as much extra knowledge about the MBS as possible, from as many sources as possible! The more information we have, the more well-rounded our opinion can be.

Alright, so you just collected a bunch of information, now what are you supposed to do about it? Easy, you act on it. You checked in and did a simple scan of your MBS, and now you have leads on where to further investigate. The following chapters will explore what to do when we find a bad vibe, but we aren't going to discuss what to do about the good stuff, necessarily. If you found something good, let that thing take the attention from the things that bring discomfort. This isn't a treatment for the bad vibes or their causes, but it is a fantastic way to deal with the fallout from them, such as stress.

EXERCISE NINE
Pendulum Scan

The practice of dowsing with a pendulum is one that I find to be underrated by many. Pendulums help us hack the conscious mind and go straight to the subconscious, which is where the MBS like to hang out. As psychic sensitives, it can be difficult to navigate the inner sky, so using a pendulum or tarot, as you are about to see, can help us get straight to the heart of the matter.

With pendulums, there are a limited number of responses that we can receive and each of those is actually the result of the combined frequency coming from you and the material the pendulum is made of. Since we each respond differently to things like stones, metal, and wood, each pendulum speaks a different type of language to each of us. What is yes to me when using a pendulum might be no for you when you work with the same piece.

The foolproof way is to check each time you pick up a pendulum and get the code set before you start asking serious questions. Unless we are dowsing over something like a crystal grid, a pendulum board, or a map, we are limited as to the answers the pendulum can provide, which means we have to ask our questions carefully. When you pick up the pendulum, hold it by the fob and allow the weight at the end to dangle from the chain or string freely without moving.

Ask it to show you what the answer *yes* is and wait for a response. Then tell it to stop. Next, ask it what *no* looks like and wait for a response, then tell it to stop again. Finally, ask it to show you what it looks like when the answer is *inconclusive*. Then, like before, tell it to stop. Each time it should cease movement before you tell it to show you the next answer. Later we will evolve our pendulum skills, but for now we really are just collecting intel.

Before we get started with the scan, ask it the following series of test questions and feel free to add your own! We do this just to make sure everything is working properly, if these are not correct then you should consider working with another pendulum.

1. Do I call myself (insert name here)?
   —*Answer should be yes.*

2. Do I live inside a public fountain?
   —*Answer should hopefully be no.*

3. Is my favorite food (insert favorite food here)?
   —*Answer should be yes.*

Now you can begin your scan. This is simple, you just need to ask the following questions and record the answers.

1. Is my body in alignment?

2. Is my body physically safe?

3. Is my body in need of attention?

4. Is my mind balanced?

5. Is my mind cloudy?

6. Is my mind in need of attention?

7. Is my spirit in alignment?

8. Is my spirit shining bright?

9. Is my spirit in need of attention?

When you are done, follow up with anything that draws attention. For example, if the answer was no to question three, it would be a good idea to follow up with more questions such as "Is my immunity compromised?" or "Do I need to adjust my diet?" Remember, all we are going to get from them using this method is *yes, no,* and *inconclusive,* so you need to ask your questions carefully.

EXERCISE TEN
Scanning with Tarot

I love the tarot and find it useful for just about all of my psychic clarity needs. Whenever I don't understand something; need to speak directly to a spirit and our connection is cloudy; or want a quick, detailed, and focused scan, I pick up my cards. Truthfully, tarot can be replaced by runes, stones, or any other form of divination that you are comfortable with or drawn to. I will be demonstrating using the tarot, but the spreads I share can just as easily be used with any other draw/lot system.

Unfortunately, I don't have the space here to give you a quick lesson on the tarot outside of the following cheat sheet. Decks usually come with their own pamphlet or booklet that explain the art and theme of the design, as well as definitions for each card. If you grab a deck without one, there are plenty of books from experts who can fill in the blanks for you.

The tricky work for any reading is in the way the cards and their meanings are interpreted, as both are highly influenced by the focus of the session. The potential outcomes are vast, so I wanted to give you a cheat sheet for interpreting any Rider-Waite-Smith deck when the focus or intent of the reading is to discover information about bad vibes. Coupled with the right layout or spread, the possibilities are endless.

Without diving into tarot theory and history, here is a brief reference for each card.

THE MAJOR ARCANA

0—The Fool: Youthful, misguided, or unintentional energy.

1—The Magician: Intended and direct energy meant for a specific purpose. Might indicate an act of magic or spiritual influence.

2—The High Priestess: Mental energy, secrets, following intuition. Might indicate a poltergeist or unintentionally sent vibes.

3—The Empress: Well-intended energy, archetypal motherly, and abundant. Can also mean Source.

4—The Emperor: Structured and harsh energy, archetypally fatherly, and restrictive. Can indicate Source and inheritance.

5—The Hierophant: Religious or systemic energy. Can also indicate a shallow understanding that lacks experience or intuition.

6—The Lovers: Partnerships, anchors, and energetic connections. Can indicate method energy travels from person to person and can also indicate spiritual influence and overshadowing.

7—The Chariot: Movement, progression, and change as well as attention to resources. Often indicates influences from spirits.

8—Strength: Inner conviction and willpower to overcome. Can indicate personal struggle and stress.

9—The Hermit: Retreating into the self and deep thoughts. Can indicate depression or anxiety and shutting ourselves off from the world. A portent of potential spiritual influence and overshadowing.

10—The Wheel of Fortune: Divine influence and fate, often indicates major spiritual activity and should be taken as a sign to take action.

11—Justice: Law, the legal system, and retribution. Indicates a need for protection.

12—The Hanged Man: Confusion and self-sabotage. Can indicate energy is stuck or unwilling to move. Cleansing and transmutation are essential.

13—Death: Main definition are endings and residual energy. While rarer, it can indicate a human spirit or literal death. Cleansing and transmutation are essential.

14—Temperance: Balancing and redistribution or resources, often indicates land spirit activity and other natural fluctuations of energy. A key portent for transmutation.

15—The Devil: Addiction and cycles of abuse. Indicates spiritual influence or overshadowing, potentially possession. Can also indicate generational curses.

16—The Tower: Destruction, anger, rage, and violent transformation. Can indicate human-caused problems, especially in cases involving homes and other physical locations.

17—The Star: Peace, hope, and serenity. Indicates absolution and divine connection. A portent of positive spiritual influence.

18—The Moon: Deception, instinct, and psychic/spiritual influence. Can indicate lower-level spirit activity or intentional deceit.

19—The Sun: Happiness and divine authority, positive spiritual influence. Can also indicate summoned divine intervention.

20—Judgment: Awakening, redemption, and transition. Indicates spirit activity and places importance on psychic/spiritual abilities.

21—The World: Completion and success. Indicates positive spiritual influences and also can direct us to look at the past or past lives for answers.

THE MINOR ARCANA

	SWORDS Thoughts and Deeds	WANDS Motivation and Passion
Ace	Clear thought and insight. Indicates psychic ability.	Spark of life, sexual energy. Indicates a lower-level spirit.
Two	Seeking internal balance. Indicates potential for overshadowing.	Tunnel vision and need for external insight.
Three	Depression, anxiety, and internal conflict. Indicates spirit activity and potential overshadowing.	Unmoving, strongly rooted.
Four	Withdrawal and healing. Indicates positive spiritual influence trying to break through.	Harmony and family.
Five	Humiliation and unresolved conflict. Unfinished business.	Strife and frustration. Can indicate competitiveness.
Six	Need for science and logic. Overweighing of the emotional, spiritual, and energetic.	Victory and self-confidence.
Seven	Schemes, trickery, and theft.	Aggression, over-reactiveness, and need for attention.
Eight	Confusion, helplessness, restriction. Indicates overshadowing.	Progression at all costs, blinded by passion, going with the flow. Indicates intentional spiritual attack or the need to shield from attack.
Nine	Sleeplessness, worry, anxiety, indicates negative spiritual entanglement.	Guarded. Indicates a strong need for protection.
Ten	Need for action. Potential possession, overshadowing. Must confront problem before it's too late.	Oppression and adversity. Indicates depression and potential spirit attachment or negative link to past.
Page	Quick intelligence that overcomes opposition.	Loyalty and eagerness.
Knight	Bravery and unstoppable ingenuity.	Adventuring, the discovery of new things.
Queen	Total honesty and direct focus with attention to detail. Indicates the need for long-term psychic protection.	Powerful confidence, self-assuredness, love for life.
King	Strong-minded, brilliant, and quick-witted. Powerful psychic abilities. Indicates a spiritual activity coming from a singular person.	Strong willed, intolerant of weakness. Indicates overshadowing.

CUPS
Emotion and Intuition

Love and new relationships.
Indicates intuitive ability.

Personal connection and
emotional investment.

Joy and friendship,
overwriting negative psychic
energy with positive.

Feeling unfulfilled and under
stimulated. Can indicate
poltergeist activity.

Emotional upset and
attention to the negative. Can
indicate overshadowing.

Nostalgia and childhood. Can
indicate the need for protection
or spirit ally communication.

Overstimulation, confusion,
and lack of movement.

Moving on, letting go,
indicates a spirit that is
seeking assistance.

Choosing pleasure over
adversity, gluttony, accepting
things as they are.

Happiness and satiety.
All is well.

Psychic and spiritual
development, potential
dormant abilities.

Psychic vision, dreams, and
messages from the other side.

Celebration, love, and
sensuality. Indicates the
need for regular spiritual
connection with allies.

Emotional maturity, artistic
expression, and a sign of
evident empathic abilities.

PENTACLES
Finances and Material Possessions

Reality and nature.
Indicates land energy.

Mixed desires, imbalance
of spiritual and physical.

Obtaining something
through skill. Indicates a
need for further discussion/
attention to detail.

Lack of security, energy
hoarding, can indicate the
source of a problem.

Suffering, a powerful bond
between people who suffer
together. Indicates residual
energy and spirit attachment.

Sharing and redistribution.
Positive energy, a break
from the negative.

Fear of failure, dissatisfaction.

New skills, need for patience,
and risk of losing focus.

Property. Deserved
contentment.

Security and relief.

Sense of wonder and
excitement for new things.

Uncomplaining resolve,
self-assuredness.

Physical beauty, pride
in the home. Sharing
positive energy freely.

Happiness, success, and
the manifestation of the
spiritual into the physical.

USING TAROT SPREADS

For the most part, we use spreads, or templated card layouts, to help us focus on specific areas of interest. Each card is placed in a specific area with a unique meaning, think of them as a location where something is happening. When a card is placed in that position, it represents the activity happening in that location. For example, in a three-card spread where the first card represents the past, the second the present, and the third the future, the fool card placed in the first position would represent a new beginning in the past.

The more you work with tarot, the easier this will be. For our purposes, we are going to be specifically focusing on the MBS. Use the following spread and record the information in your journal.

1	2	3
4	5	6
7	8	9

Here are the placement and meanings for this spread:

1–2: Supporting Details—Information related to the state of the spirit.

3: A summary of the body's current state of being.

4–5: Supporting Details—Information related to the state of the mind.

6: A summary of the mind's current state of being.

7–8: Supporting Details—Information related to the state of the body.

9: A summary of the body's current state of being.

AFTER THE SCAN

As I said earlier, what we do with this information is up to us, but we should have a pretty good idea of where we are in life based on what we collected here. We should have enough to go on and investigate for years to come, likely only scratching the surface as to what the MBS has to share. All of that takes time and some of the information you collect might not be particularly useful to you, especially in the moment. Recording it is still a good idea, as you never know when that information might be useful at another time. More so than that, however, knowing all this is one thing, but doing something about it is another altogether.

If you found good things and good vibes in your scan, let those things remind you that it isn't all bad. Life includes suffering but isn't made of it. If you found some things about yourself that you need to work on, then welcome to the club! If, however, you discovered that you are in fact being disturbed by bad vibes, then the following chapters are going to help deal with what ails you.

SPIRIT ALLIES

Last but not least, lets dive into what might be my favorite topic in this whole book, that of spirit guides and the spirit partnerships we can develop to help us be all we can be. As a professional medium of more than twenty years, I am here to tell you that you have a spirit sitting on your shoulder at this very moment. It's okay to look, go ahead, I'll wait.

I am mentioning spirit allies early on because mine are part of my system for approaching any type of bad vibration. Not only do they know things before I do but they also have the skinny on a lot of what is happening on the spiritual/psychic highway. Developing a partnership with your own, regardless of how skilled at mediumship you might be, will only make the whole scanning and preparing aspect of what we do easier.

Spirit allies are the spirits that we work with (consciously and subconsciously) who are directly invested in our highest good because they are directly tied to our Higher Selves. I know that sounds utterly silly, but they are real, I promise. Depending on who you are, that spirit can be something akin to an angel, perhaps a deceased loved one, or even someone you've met between lives.

These spirits might look like a person, like an animal or a mythical creature, or like no living thing at all, and all of this depends on your connection to them and their true nature. The best part is, they are there whether we acknowledge them or not, and they will always have your back to the best of their ability. The closer we are to them intentionally, the more influence they can have, which means the more help you get.

Now, if you are a pragmatist, you might be asking yourself what these spirits get out of the whole thing, and the answer might surprise you.

To spirits, corporeal existence is a precious commodity. Not because all spirits want to come through as embodied entities but because physical existence is the most efficient way to produce energy. Energy that everything, living and nonliving, needs to exist. If you can't manifest physically, the next best thing is to connect to a living thing and essentially use their physicality secondhand. This is why spirit attachments of any kind occur. The spirit needs energy, and whether that is coming through you directly or ambiently, you are still the best avenue for them to pursue.

Spirit guides are spirits that work with us beneficially, but they are, in a sense, still a form of spirit attachment; just one that we prefer. It is in their best interest to keep you alive, happy, and thriving because that way they get more of what they need. It is important to remember that all of us have spirit attachments and that we are designed to. We know this because the plugs to do so come with the basic human hardware package. Any medium can tell you that when they peek behind the curtain that everyone has at least one extra someone with them at any given moment.

Sometimes we make these arrangements before we are embodied, which is the case with several of the guides I work with. However, I also have a few guides that I have picked up along the way. It is normal for guides to come and go out of our lives and for those of us who embrace our psychic and spiritual abilities have multiple guides. It is also common for ancestors to take the place of a guide until we are old enough to make new connections. I believe this is why we have so many stories of deceased loved ones checking in on babies.

Spirit guides help themselves by helping us, which makes them invested in things such as our happiness and health. This means they make excellent partners when doing things like shadow work, but also when navigating the world in general. This is especially true when working against bad vibes, regardless of where they are coming from. Having a working relationship with your guides can be a massive help when working on yourself and when battling bad vibes elsewhere.

EXERCISE ELEVEN
Meeting Your Guides, Part One

Use this exercise to meet your guides, or to clarify your connection with them if you already have a sense of who they are. To do this, all you need is something to write your thoughts down in.

Begin by finding somewhere comfortable to sit. Then, close your eyes and bring your focus to your breath. Release any distractions and allow your mind to settle into those moments of stillness and silence at the beginning and end of each breath. If you find yourself becoming distracted at any point during this exercise, return your thoughts to those points of stillness and silence.

Close your eyes and visualize yourself alone in the space that you feel the most comfortable in. This could be your bedroom, your office, your car, or any other space that brings you a sense of belonging and purpose. Take a few moments to fill in the details and then visualize a piece of paper, an envelope, and a pen in your hands. Using the pen, write a message to your guides. If you are currently working on something in your life and need help with something specific, then write a message about that, otherwise (or additionally) write, "meet me here tomorrow." Fold the paper up, put it in the envelope, then write "Spirit Guides" on it and leave it somewhere obvious in the space.

Take three deep breaths, gently bring your mind back into your body with each exhale, and release the visualization. Open your eyes and jot down your impressions about this space if you have any. Did you feel another presence there with you?

EXERCISE TWELVE
Meeting Your Guides, Part Two

To complete the exercise, we are going to revisit this space as we did in part one, this time with the expectation that our guides will make themselves known. You have created the space, you have left the message, now it is time for them to do their thing. This time when you go back to the space, allow the visualization to fill itself in on its own, paying attention to details that have changed since its construction in your mind the day before.

Hopefully your guides are chatty and are simply there waiting for you. If that is the case, then start talking. I have a set of questions for you to ask at the end of this exercise. If your guides like to play hide-and-seek, like mine, then zero in on any shifts to the space that you notice and investigate them. These are clues as to who your guides are and where to find them. We aren't all hardwired the same, and it is possible that not all the wiring is properly hooked up in the first place. These subtle shifts are like threads, pull them to see what they unravel. This might take a few attempts, but those are almost certainly the keys you're looking for.

Keep in mind that your guides could look like anything or anyone. Mine famously show up as animals, digital characters, and even as figurines on a shelf. Your mind is weird, this process is weird, and all of that spiritual information has to filter through both, so just go with the flow. You might need to leave another note and come back the next day, that is okay. For some reason it is super easy for me to talk to dead people, but I struggled to meet my guides in the beginning. That changes, of course, but it might take time.

Once you encounter one (or more), it is time to play ten questions. This is super important because it helps you to build a profile of them that will become invaluable as you battle bad vibes together. After you ask each question, open your eyes and jot the response you're given in your journal. Take a breath, close your eyes, return to the space, and ask the next one. Eventually, you'll be able to be in both places at once, able to communicate with your guides in your mind while still actively engaging your environment without letting on to others that you are doing so. This is a skill that develops with practice, however. In the beginning it is best to take it slow and to fully appreciate the value of each response.

Like the spirits themselves, the answers may not come clearly. You might see an image or hear a sound instead of getting a straightforward response. That's also perfectly normal, just write down what you see.

TEN QUESTIONS TO ASK A SPIRIT GUIDE

1. What is your name?

2. Are you here for my highest good?

3. What are you here to help me with?

4. What do you get out of the experience of working with me?

5. How long have you been working with me?

6. What are the shapes or forms you might take?

7. Is there an area of my life that needs attention right now?

8. How best can I serve myself right now?

9. How do I know when you are reaching out to me?

10. How would you like me to reach out to you?

The golden rule is to always allow for nuance with each of the answers except for the second one. If the response you get to "Are you here for my highest good?" is anything other than yes, it's time to close up shop and reboot the experiment with a clearer understanding of part one. Somehow wires got crossed and you stumbled onto what is likely just spiritual wildlife (more on that in chapter 5) or at the very least a spirit that you can't trust, which means it's not a guide, just something pretending to be one.

Once you have the answers, you can formulate a method of contact with your guide, and it will be easier to anchor them into your life. End the exercise as you did in part one. From there, the sky is the limit.

It is generally a good idea to pay attention to your dreams and daydreams, which is most likely where those points of contact will happen. It's normal for them to reach out in real life as well, which is always a bit odd and synchronistic. For some, it's having a guide that comes to them in the form of a panther and seeing a giant panther painted on the side of a truck while they are running errands. For me, it's usually songs or noises. For example, I hear one of my favorite bands pop up randomly on a radio playlist or over the speaker when I'm out shopping. Eventually, you will establish your own strange language with your guides and allies. Follow your gut, revisit the space, hold meetings with your guides when needed, and be open to the possibilities.

We will revisit spirit guides in later chapters. For now, work on developing a strong relationship with them and let them show you the way forward. Whenever you have a question about a vibration you sense, or when you encounter a vibration for the first time, inquire with your guides about their thoughts and advice.

CONCLUSION AND JOURNALING

Once we can get over the initial shock or weirdness of accepting that we are psychic/spiritual beings, the possibilities suddenly become endless. Yes, we feel and sense vibrations, but we can also follow our senses to the cause of those vibrations, and if need be, we can do something about them. We can't, however, do anything about those vibrations if we are unable to figure out what they are and where they are coming from. The techniques we discussed here will go a long way in helping you to discern that information.

This chapter was all about discovering different ways to identify the vibrations around and within us. We will, of course, continue to develop these skills throughout the book, but much of what we discuss here can be immediately applied to any situation. Before we move on, take a few minutes to respond to the following journal prompts as openly and honestly as possible.

1. How do you feel about using your psychic gifts after reading the last two chapters? Is it something you feel confident about? If not, what would help you become confident?

2. Have you worked with a pendulum before? If so what kind and what was the experience like?

3. How do you feel about the tarot? Have you worked with it before? If so, what was the experience like? If not, what do you think it will be like and why?

4. What were your preconceptions about spirit guides before reading this chapter? After meeting them, do you feel they lived up to those preconceptions or was the experience different from what you were expecting?

5. What are three techniques that were discussed in this chapter that you found valuable or inspiring?

6. Using the information we have discussed in the last two chapters, come up with a quick action plan for how you will approach bad vibrations in the future.

(((PART TWO)))
BAD VIBRATIONS

By the time I was fifteen, I had already had more than my fair share of the strange and unusual popping into my life, and I was eager to learn as much as I could about the spiritual and the psychic. I wanted to figure out not only what I was capable of but also what exactly I was experiencing. It was the peak of my impressionable phase, and let's just say that I am thankful Tik-Tok wasn't around back then or I would have made some pretty embarrassing videos and no one would ever take me seriously. I wanted to believe just about every story, and I was more than willing to give people the benefit of the doubt as I scoured message boards and blogs looking for every ounce of information I could and any story that would reveal itself.

My interest peaked that summer when my cousin made the evening news for barely escaping an attack by a local cryptid known as the Frog Man. The Frog Man had been in the area supposedly for hundreds of years and there were stories about it that predated the settlers in the area. According to her, she and a friend had been out playing in the woods when they encountered the beast, and it chased them for quite some time before they were able to lose it. The story was an overnight sensation, and people came from all over the country to join the search for the Frog Man.

It took a few weeks, but eventually interest died down and life went back to normal. Well, normal for most people, but our grandmother passed away. It was sad of course, but while staying with my family during the service, I had the opportunity to talk with my cousin in person about the Frog Man.

"We made it all up," she said bitterly. "It isn't a big deal. Mom already knows."

I remember not knowing how to respond to that. Instead, I twisted my face in confusion. She looked up and noticed my awkward grimace and then filled in some of the blanks.

"You want to know why? I don't know. We just got carried away and then one thing led to another. We did feel something watching us, but we weren't chased and there is no such thing as the Frog Man."

I was devastated. I wanted so badly for her story to be true, but it wasn't, and she was probably right, there was no such thing as the Frog Man. That was the day that I learned the most valuable lesson of them all: always be a skeptic, especially if you are a believer.

In part 2, we are going to examine bad vibrations and the things we perceive as negative. We will start with a good look in the mirror and then slowly work our way outward to the vibrations of other people, and then eventually to those of locations and the preternatural. Chances are, if it gives you the creeps or makes you feel spiritually uncomfortable, we will cover it here.

HOW TO USE THIS SECTION

The next three chapters focus on explaining what the bad vibes we might be dealing with are and provide a handful of exercises for confronting them. Parts three and four focus specifically on confronting these vibrations, so I chose not to fill each of these chapters with that information. Instead, you will find entries on a wide range of spiritual, psychic, and preternatural topics.

You will notice that at the start of the majority of entries I list a "Disturbance Level" that ranges from one to five. This information corresponds with the Scale of Cleansing, which we will go over in chapters 7 and 8. As you might guess, that number correlates to the potential severity and threat level of that particular disturbance; however, it isn't particularly valuable outside of the intended context.

3

OUR BAD VIBES

In the previous chapter, we looked at how vibrations work and what bad vibrations want from us. In this chapter, we are going to take a shame-free dive into the ways we can sometimes cause the bad vibrations in our lives and what to do about it. We are also going to take our first look at the potential issues that can arise when we don't allow for our vital energies to ground and center properly.

For those who are looking at all of this with a fresh pair of eyes, you will find a set of practices that don't seem spiritual at surface level but can (and will) have profound effects on your capability as a spiritual being and as a psychic. The experienced psychic sensitive will find key areas that are potential trouble spots for them and their fellow sensitives to keep an eye out for when battling personal bad vibes.

We are our own worst enemy. I probably don't need to tell you that; I bet you have at least a dozen examples of how you have gotten in your own way in the past. It is one of those hallmarks of being a human and comes with the territory. In addition to my fair share of self-sabotage, I have also been helping people deal with their own since I started working as a professional psychic. What no one tells you when you sign up for the gig is that people tend to go to psychics over going to a therapist, and I have found myself in more than one instance where I took on the role of spiritual counselor. Of all the hats I wear, spiritual counselor is my favorite.

Keep in mind that I am no therapist or psychiatrist, and what I say here is not meant to be a substitute for seeing either. In fact, I am one of those weird spiritual counselors who highly recommends to all his clients that they see a mental health professional as a matter of healthy living. For clients who seek me out for exorcisms or similar work, I require them to see a therapist of their choice afterward at least three times as part of their aftercare. This requirement tends to keep those out for attention from knocking on my door and helps my clients know that I take mental health seriously, even as a weirdo who talks to invisible people.

Most people don't realize there is a major connection between mental and spiritual health. It makes sense when you take a step back, and those who have studied psychology are fully aware of the link. We can't focus on either for too long before running into the other. For the psychically sensitive, that connection takes on a third dimension. We not only sense the energy we come in contact with, we interact with it as well. Like sponges, we absorb whatever we are dipped into and then gush it back out when we are squeezed.

As a bit of a side note, it is my opinion that if we truly seek spiritual clarity, we need a little therapy from time to time. Spiritual counseling can do many of the same things therapy can offer; however, people like me aren't equipped to deal with some of the bigger stuff that might come up. You got ghosts in your basement? Sure, give me a call. But the ones in your head require a very different type of guidance to resolve. Anyway, all this to say therapy is for everyone, especially the psychically sensitive.

You didn't come here for therapy; you came for all the spiritual stuff, and lucky for both of us, I am fully capable of being your guide through these waters. Before we go any further, I want to make one thing abundantly clear: Just because the bad vibes we discuss here might come from you or have been attracted to you, that doesn't mean it's your fault. My real hope is that as we move through the following topics the information here helps you not only resolve some of your own issues but also helps to build a better understanding of how these vibrations, and their affects, manifest in the world around you.

Bad things (and bad vibes) happen to innocent people every day; that doesn't mean it is their fault. By no means am I trying to victim blame or shame; my intention is to give those who are victims a few tools to turn the tables. Remember what I said in the introduction: I believe you; I also believe you picked up this book because you wanted to create real change.

THE SPIRITUAL EFFECTS OF STRESS, TRAUMA, AND DEPRESSION

I mentioned earlier that there is a connection between the mental and the spiritual. This works as you might expect: the healthier you are in mind, the healthier you'll be in spirit. The same can be said for physical health, as well. The mind-body-spirit connection is a very real thing, and there is a reason so many spiritual authors talk about it in one form or another.

Bringing those three pieces of ourselves into harmony is a means to true wholeness, connection, and purpose. We talk about being in alignment and finding balance as a means to this harmony a lot in metaphysical books, but we rarely discuss what happens when those adjustments aren't made. What happens when the mind, body, and spirit aren't allowed to find harmony and we aren't allowed to be whole.

THE MIND-BODY-SPIRIT CONNECTION

The body and the spirit communicate through instinct, the body and the mind through our drives and impulses, but nothing is quite as dynamic as the connection between the mind and the spirit. This bond creates our perception of reality, and reality is where we spend every moment of our lives.

Our bodies have a whole lot to do with how we perceive reality as well. Our body moves through the physical space of our realities and our health and wellness are directly tied to our mental health. Reality is, as you can see, a somewhat fragile thing, and our ability to interact with it varies at different times in our lives, depending on the health and functionality of those three parts.

Many spiritual types, myself included, believe that a human's natural state is to be in harmony with their environment and, by proxy, have a healthy life that lends to a balanced form of personal reality. That is to say, we aren't supposed to be miserable, unhappy, or stressed, and that is why so many of us strive to better our personal condition as a way of life. Exercise, art, and social connections are all ways we strive to give ourselves a happy life. Sometimes, we can't quite land comfortably in reality and reach for short-term solutions.

When we take drugs or experience an internal chemical shift, the way we perceive reality is altered through physical means, and our spirit-mind connection is altered, if only for the duration of the experience. The temporary relief drugs and alcohol might provide, however, are still only masking the root problem of our disturbance.

Historically, we turn to drugs and alcohol, and even spirituality, to help us cope with underlying struggles in our lives. For the most part, we can oversimplify and boil these struggles down to stress, depression, and trauma. Because the mind, body, and spirit are connected, these three can cause a lot of trouble if left to grow on their own.

The truth is that when we get down to the nitty-gritty of it, stress, depression, and trauma are hard to distinguish between because they carry a lot of the same symptoms. Stress is often described as an internal pressure that builds up over time, depression tends to come with a lot of sedentary thoughts and behavior, and trauma is understood to be scarring left with us after we experience something deeply disturbing or painful. As you can guess, there is often a lot of overlap with the three, and they can present themselves to varying degrees at any point in our lives.

In addition to these things effecting the way we construct and interact with reality, they can construct and interact with other planes of awareness as well. On occasion, pieces of ourselves even carry the weight of other lifetimes.

PAST LIVES

Sometimes the stress, depression, and trauma we experience in a past life influences how we live this one. I admit that I was skeptical for a long time, especially being someone who talked to dead people, but over time I eventually became a convert.

One of the main focuses of past-life regression is to heal trauma from a previous life that is impacting your current one. I frequently recommend clients and students undergo therapeutic past-life regression with a hypnotherapist to clear up blockages and heal emotional wounds. Past-life regression has a lot to offer us aside from healing, however. The insight we gain from these experiences can cue us in to why we find resistance in certain areas in this life and help us conquer them.

Before publishing my first book, I was quite unsure about my life as a writer. I had at least a dozen unfinished manuscripts, and I couldn't seem to complete them. I was fortunate in that I was one of those writers who had both interest in my work and opportunity to work for some excellent companies, and I didn't want to waste them. This was something I had struggled with for years and it had become a big issue that I battled with in secret.

When I got my first book deal, I knew I was in for a rude awakening and time was soon running out. By some divine grace, I got a random text from a friend who needed my help with one of her final exams. She was finishing her hypnotherapy certification and needed to lead someone through a past-life regression in front of her mentor and record the session to present to the rest of her class. She told me I only needed to come with a problem I'd like to resolve in mind.

The session was much different than I expected. I had done past-life regressions before under the direction of more than one spiritual teacher, but they always had a motive or a reason for wanting to look at a particular life. This wasn't anything like that. We let the problem take me to the lifetime where it originated.

I found myself back in a city that I think was either New York or Chicago during prohibition. I was a reporter doing a story related to bootlegging and was taken out after being led into a trap by an informant. I was supposed to have the story turned in to my editor that afternoon but was never able to do so.

When I tell you that the last thing I ever expected to see was me being shot in an alley sometime in the 1920s, I could not be more serious. The whole experience was matter-of-fact and almost like being inside a movie. At the time, nothing felt unhinged or resolved, but I did find myself suddenly able to finish my manuscript after. I also went looking for stories that matched the one I saw and found dozens. Apparently, it wasn't so uncommon during that time to end up swimming with the fishes when you looked where you weren't supposed to during those times. Unfortunately, I couldn't get enough details to make a match with any deaths on record.

What came out of that experience was a belief that I was far more complicated than I could imagine and that I probably had the means to work through all of my major obstacles in life, even if it meant looking at a previous one for answers. It also had the side effect of freeing me from whatever had been inhibiting the completion of my book, and it helped me recover a missing piece. If you find yourself in a situation where you are repeatedly running into the same issue in life and can't seem to overcome it, I recommend reaching out to a trained hypnotherapist and doing a past-life regression. In my case, it was a total game changer.

FINDING RELIEF

I am just going to say it: you have to work on yourself. It isn't groundbreaking, nor is it necessarily exciting. The only way to keep from being the problem in your own life is to look within and do whatever healing is needed so you feel confident and whole. In the spiritual world, we call this *shadow work*, which is essentially a woo-woo term for self-improvement by confronting the mental and emotional things that haunt us. Don't get me wrong, it isn't necessarily a simple process, but the aim is quite clear: take back your power. Sometimes this means reading a few self-help books and talking to your friends about your life, and other times it means going to therapy, working with a professional, or maybe even going on retreat.

The focus is to help you strip away the vibes that you've picked up, or developed, that are keeping you from feeling good about where you are now and where you are headed. Because the mind and the spirit are so intertwined, whatever we do to help our mental state will have a direct effect on our spiritual one, and vice versa. This also means that we need to treat them in tandem, and I find the best way to do this is to bring the body into the conversation. Where the mind and the spirit fail to communicate, the body can be our translator. Pay close attention to your physical response to the mental and the spiritual things happening in your life. If you notice any of the bad-vibe effects that we talked about in the previous chapter, chances are it is a great place to bring focus in your personal work.

We all need to do shadow work, in my opinion, but this is especially true for those who are psychic sensitives. Remember, our gifts work both ways, and our shadow is part of us. This means that our shadow can make the decisions about not only what spiritual frequencies we are tuning in to but also what frequencies and vibrations we are projecting out into the world. The shadow can be responsible for a lot of bad vibes, those created and self-imposed, those that are attracted to you, and otherwise. Let's discuss the shadow self in a bit more detail.

SHADOW WORK AND THE SHADOW SELF

This is another one of those topics that I wish I had the space to fully explore with you. To do so would truly be a monumental task, however, and no two of us are the same, so strategy and approach will vary. I've included a few recommended books on the topic in the bibliography and recommended reading for those of you who wish to further dive into the topic. I will outline here one approach that I find myself returning to often for personal use and when working with my clients.

The *shadow self* is the part of us that we don't want to see. The term was coined by famous psychologist and researcher Carl Jung to describe the unconscious components of our personality that we reject. These aspects are (mostly) rooted in our childhood and adolescence and spring forth from interactions that diminish us or make us feel insecure but can occur at any time in life.

A good example would be getting in a car accident when you are a child and as a result you avoid getting your driver's license as an adult, to the point of it interfering with your ability to find gainful employment. Another would be being scolded as a child for not eating all the food on your plate and then developing an unhealthy relationship with food as a result that causes health concerns later in life. Or how about my personal favorite, being told you were too loud as a child and then finding it hard to speak your mind as an adult.

These are basic examples, but hopefully you are catching my drift. The shadow self is part of you, it isn't something that can be exorcised or removed, nor should you want to. Each of its pieces are rooted in you and to rid yourself of them would only lead to further harm. The objective with shadow work is to confront them, find their cause, heal that cause, and then integrate what is left back into your psyche. Depending on what we are looking at, the work required for each of those steps will differ.

Shadow work requires critical and objective thinking, which not all of us are great at, and this is why so many seek out a counselor, a priest, a shaman, or a therapist to help them go as deep as possible. You can do it alone, or at least get started alone, and incorporate the help of others once you reach a matter that you want to explore further with assistance.

EXERCISE THIRTEEN
Self Shadow Work

To do shadow work on your own, get a journal or set up a file on your computer where you can journal. So much of what we need to do in the beginning is map out our thoughts and sort out our emotions, which journaling is perfect for.

If you aren't sure where to begin your shadow work journey, check out the exercises from the previous chapter, which should provide some idea of where to put your attention. If you are still unsure, here are five journaling prompts to help you reflect on your shadow and how it might be affecting your life and vibration. Respond as honestly as possible but remember that you don't get points for being too self-deprecating or for misleading yourself. If it helps, think of yourself as a client during the evaluation process.

1. Are there aspects of your life that you feel too ashamed of to share with people you love? What are those aspects and what actions are taken to avoid discussing them? How does your need to keep these things a secret effect your mood when you are around those people?

2. When was the last time you withheld information or your opinion because you weren't comfortable? What happened to you as a result of withholding your opinion? How did that affect your relationship with others?

3. List three pet peeves you have. What are the earliest memories you have about those pet peeves? How do they affect your ability to relate to others?

4. List one to three people who you struggle to get along with. What assumptions do you have about them and their behavior? Why?

5. When was the last time you lied and what was the lie about? Why did you choose to mislead others? How does misleading people make you feel about your self-worth?

CONFRONTING WHAT YOU FIND

This set of questions is designed to bring stuff up so you can be aware of the underlining support structure of the shadow self. The goal at this point is to rest with that awareness and then use it to help make better decisions that empower you. Even if those are subtle shifts, each shift matters, and over time, they create massive shifts.

Don't feel the need to take it all on at once, either. It is perfectly acceptable to pick one thing and start there before moving on. I recommend clients pick something different each day that came up while journaling and work on that. Keep rotating through until you feel like you have more ability in that area. Or, alternatively, pick one or two things and work on those for a week.

HEALING AND INTEGRATING THE SHADOW

After you have confronted the aspects of yourself that comprise and support the shadow self, it is time to give extra special attention to the things you are good at, the things that bring you confidence and happiness, and the things that help you feel good about yourself. I'm not talking about ice cream; I'm talking about the parts of yourself that you love. When we are faced with all of our shitty qualities, it is extra important to remember the good ones. Not only will this give us a needed boost of confidence when confronting the not-so-good but doing so will also give us an idea of what tools we have at our disposal to confront those things. For example, I love art and being creative, and I use art (something I feel confident in) to help me confront my shadow by painting or doodling my feelings and thoughts. I have a friend who enjoys exercise and uses her workout sessions to burn through her shadow blocks. Our goal here is to heal through confidence and, most importantly, acceptance.

Integrating the shadow is a life-long process, it isn't something we do and then walk away from. The shadow is always going to be there, but the hope is that it isn't the one driving the car; instead, we want for your better-adjusted side to be in control. Each time you are confronted with a situation where the shadow could take the wheel, remind yourself that you are vulnerable and then reaffirm your commitment to creating change in that area.

LEVELS OF DISTURBANCE

Shadow work is a form of cleansing. Depending on how deep you go, you can potentially end up performing what is the equivalent to a level four cleansing on our nifty scale (more in chapters 7 and 8). If you find yourself reaching a point of overwhelm, reach out for help—be it from a professional, someone you know, or even your spirit guides and allies.

Quantifying the level of disturbance when it comes to personal vibration is difficult because the degree of intensity experienced can differ greatly depending on circumstance. Most of the time, we are looking at a level one type, but if the person is a strong psychic (compared to the average person) then we could easily be looking at a level three type of disturbance. As a matter of personal spiritual hygiene, especially for the psychically sensitive, shadow work should be a regular practice. Not only does it help the psychic better understand their internal struggles but also how those struggles may be manifesting outside themselves. Let's look at the scale.

« *UNTRAINED PSYCHIC ABILITY* »
Disturbance Level: 1–5

As I mentioned at the start, we are all psychic and spiritually connected to the greater Universe, some of us just more so than others. In a world full of screens and distractions that keep us looking elsewhere, spiritual gifts often go unnoticed until there is a problem. When things do start going awry, we often don't know where to investigate because our symptoms look nothing like what they are made to look like in the movies or on television. We are led to assume psychic phenomena would be big and noticeable, but in truth, subtlety is the way of the spiritual.

Psychic experiences, good or bad, happen to us constantly, we just aren't often aware of them. The messages get jumbled up with our thoughts and we don't give them a closer look. It is in the rarest of cases that you will experience the apparition of a ghost or find yourself toe-to-toe with a demonic spirit. More often than not, you'll experience an odd mood change or a strange memory will float upward from the depths of your mind. The training, more than anything, allows us to understand the vibrations we pick up, the moment we pick them up. It helps us to sort out the meaning and the essence of the vibrations you come in contact with and prepares you to battle the forces of bad vibes when you need to.

Being psychic is not inherently a good thing or a bad thing, and what you can actually do with it depends on a cocktail of circumstance, environment, and propensity. We aren't all tuned in to the same frequency, either, and so what works for some may not work for others. Devoting time to figuring out how your psychic abilities work is half the battle. The rest will come through experience.

Untrained psychic abilities are the root cause of much of what we face as spiritual people on the front lines. I can speak from personal experience and tell you that everything got better when I took my training seriously in every single aspect of my life. Unfortunately, there is no textbook with all the answers.

For now, knowing you have all the power is enough, just be sure to do something about it.

So how do you know if your psychic abilities are getting in your way or if they might be causing bad vibes? As you might imagine, that looks different in each of us, but there are some standout characteristics. There are two areas of interest to pay attention to: the internal world and the immediate external. For most of us, untrained psychic ability comes with internal struggles, such as depression and anxiety, that are often difficult to pinpoint and explain to others. Look for obsessive/cyclical thoughts, overstimulation, and physical tiredness. In the immediate external, look for things like technology going wonky around you, lights flickering, inexplicable accidents, and my personal favorite, hearing odd noises like static.

Generally speaking, doing a level two cleansing should take care of any disturbance connected to untrained ability, provided you are working to develop your abilities. Otherwise, the disturbance will likely just come back. Of all the possible issues that could arise from having untrained abilities that we need to worry about, is the potential for poltergeists.

« POLTERGEIST »
Disturbance Level: 3–5

Over the years, I have worked with thousands of people who believed they were haunted or that there was some sort of demonic activity in their lives. Sometimes this has been true, but often the phenomena they were experiencing and attributing to an external spirit was actually the result of what is referred to in the field of paranormal studies as *poltergeist activity*.

Despite the word being German for "noisy ghost," poltergeists are what happens when those bad vibe seeds are allowed to grow in the subconscious and express themselves through our (sometimes latent) psychic abilities. Stress, depression, and trauma in the psychically gifted can be the perfect catalysts for this type of activity.

Poltergeist occur as a transference of vital energies once pressure has built up in the agent. It gets its name because this phenomenon often occurs as a knocking sound on a wall or other flat surface and sometimes even audible voices. In mild cases, it can manifest as tapping, popping, and potentially as acute levitation with small objects. In moderate instances, it is common to hear the famous knocks and whispers and for heavier items to move on their own, such as strollers, small statues, and even pots and pans. In extreme cases, however, there have been reports of everything from bodily levitation to the rearrangement of furniture, and so on.

Basically, just about anything reported in the paranormal world could, in theory, be attributed to some sort of poltergeist. While that is highly unlikely, the symptoms of even the most dreadful of paranormal phenomena always has the potential to be linked back to a psychic sensitive who is stressed, depressed, or experiencing the effects of trauma.

FINDING RELIEF

Whenever I am approaching a case where paranormal phenomena have been reported, I always consider the possibility that it might be caused by someone in the home or at the location. If this is the case, key things to know are that it will occur when the person is either highly stressed or deeply relaxed, both are times when the subconscious mind is busy at work. When the person is physically not there, the activity decreases almost entirely. The activity ends when the subconscious mind is engaged and whatever was causing the upset is identified and addressed.

Poltergeist activity is more common among those experiencing puberty and other hormonal shifts, as well as those with reoccurring post-traumatic stress. It is also more common with those who tend to be more psychically sensitive; those with a history of poltergeist activity often have latent or unexplored psychic ability.

Poltergeists are kind of like psychic spasms and, by their very nature, are something we don't necessarily control. However, also like spasms, the best way to treat them is to therapeutically engage the muscle on a regular basis, much like with stretching or yoga. Rarely is poltergeist activity witnessed with trained and developed psychics, as even the most basic psychic development exercises can engage the systems responsible for this type of activity. That being said, the more you work a muscle system without proper conditioning, the higher your chances of experiencing spasms. Likewise, even the strongest psychics among us are potential agents of poltergeist activity if they aren't properly balancing their vital energies.

In my own life, I have had more than one occurrence of this happening in some form or another, and when I was younger those experiences were traumatizing. It should be noted that the stress caused by a poltergeist can be enough to give it what it needs to proliferate. Things tend to break around me when I am stressed, including glasses, crystals, and light bulbs, sometimes before I am even conscious that I am stressed in the first place. The less I am able to take care of myself in those moments, the more likely it is that I'll break a wine glass, which really sucks when it has been a long week and all I want is a glass of wine.

Poltergeists can become very big problems if the conditions are right. If the agent is left to be a psychic pressure cooker, eventually that energy will infuse with the location and, in the rarest of cases, it can form a type of sentience. The chances of this increase if the location doesn't have a natural clearing cycle or if energy naturally pools in that location. More on how psychic energy collects in chapter 4, and we will revisit poltergeist then, as well.

CONCLUSION AND JOURNALING

We are complicated little batteries of vital energy and there are several things that can impact the way we interact with the world. Sometimes we have control over those influences, but sometimes there are unseen influences that muddy the water. I think it all really boils down to the idea that when you are off, your vibe is off, and that can cause problems that we can't pinpoint so easily. If anything, let what we discussed here be a reminder as to the importance of self-care and spiritual health.

In this chapter, we talked about the mind-body-spirit connection and how these three aspects of ourselves construct reality. We talked about what happens when that reality becomes warped and the three main causes for this warping of reality. We then took it a step further and discussed the issues that can arise as psychic agents when our reality is warped.

Before we move on, take a few minutes to respond to the following journal prompts. Be sure to answer these as honestly as possible and to the best of your ability. The more detailed and thoughtful your responses, the deeper you can take the work.

1. What are the personal symptoms you experience when you are stressed in your life on a mental, spiritual, and physical level?

2. What are the personal symptoms you experience when you are depressed in your life on a mental, spiritual, and physical level?

3. Do you carry the weight of past trauma? If so, how does it impact you on a mental, spiritual, and physical level?

4. Do you feel you have a past-life connection that might be getting in the way of something you are trying to manifest now? Do you know what that connection is?

5. We all have shadow work to do, what three elements of your shadow are you willing to tackle in order to lighten up your spiritual/psychic load?

6. What happens to your vital energies when you do not balance and ground regularly? How does that impact your ability to perceive the spiritual and the psychic?

7. Have you ever had a poltergeist experience that you accidentally caused? What were the contributing factors leading up to the experience?

4

OTHER PEOPLE'S BAD VIBES

Moving right along, we transcend the personal and now enter the realm of the communal vibrations that we are most likely to encounter. Whereas the previous chapter was all about how our spiritual energy can be affected by bad vibrations and how we ourselves can be the originators of those vibes, this chapter looks at the unique play on energies that happen when people interact with one another.

Readers who are new to all of this are going to get a crash course in psychic/spiritual connectivity and will learn how energy interacts with the world around us once it leaves a psychic agent. Those who are more experienced will find terminology put to many of the vibrations we experience but find difficult to explain, along with a few things to look out for when working on behalf of others.

OTHER PEOPLE ARE MESSY

I am one of those individuals who remains torn between wanting to fill my life with others and the extreme urge to become a forest hermit who forsakes society for trees and moss. Don't get me wrong, I believe having other people in our lives is essential to a healthy existence, it's just that connections are messy, and people are messy. Living in a rotting, hollowed-out tree stump would be a lot easier to deal with than some of the connections we come across. That all being said, empathy, love, kinship, and a deep desire for healthy community keeps us coming back for more. Yes, people are messy and they can absolutely suck sometimes, but we are people too.

We've spent the last two chapters hashing out the many ways that we can be messy. As we move forward, apply what you've learned about yourself to others. In all the ways we can create bad vibes for ourselves, others can, and are, doing the same for themselves. Absolutely no one is infallible, and everyone deserves the benefit of the doubt when assuming intent. When encountering bad vibes from others, I have learned to err on the side of empathy and stoicism.

For the most part, the messy stuff that comes from interacting, knowing, and loving other people tends to be unintentional. To quote Hanlon's razor, *"Never attribute to malice that which is adequately explained by stupidity."*

I honestly believe that most bad vibes we run into are unintentional. Life is hard, people get stuck in their heads, and we are all doing the best we can to survive. We will explore methods for counteracting these vibes later, but I don't want to give you the impression that it's all unintentional. There are people who mean us harm, wish us ill, and send out very intentional bad vibes. Sometimes these people are strangers, sometimes they are people we barely know, and sometimes they are people who are (or once were) close to us.

When the bad vibes are intentional, it is natural to feel attacked and to take it personally, but I want to caution you on this as a psychically sensitive person. For us to take something personally, we have to rationalize another person's behavior as being directly tied to something about ourselves. We are literally letting those vibes integrate themselves into aspects of our being and allowing them to take ownership of the space they consume. That just causes more of those problems we talked about in the previous chapter.

There will undoubtedly be times when you are responsible for part of the bad vibes expressed between you and another person, and it is imperative for you to own your part in the matter if you expect healing or empowerment. On the other hand, if the other person is going out of their way to create bad vibes, then that is ultimately their problem. It speaks to their state of being, not yours. Have empathy and love for others, but don't hold space for the bad vibes they create out of a sense of duty or responsibility simply because you have empathy and love. That is not rational. Put your needs first. It might sound harsh but if the plane is going down, we all know to put our mask on before helping others do the same.

Let's take a look at the different types of bad vibrations, and their causes, that happen between people, intentionally or not.

YOUR ANCHORS

Anchors are people who tie us down to aspects of our identity. They are our family, our friends, our partners, and the solid touchstones who seem to always be there one way or another. Sometimes, they only last for the moment to help us weather a storm on our way to bigger and better things (temporary anchors), sometimes they last a lifetime (permanent anchors).

It is normal for these relationships to be complex and nuanced, and I think it is safe to say that there is no one-size-fits-all model for what those relationships look like from the outside. On the inside, however, the specifics are generally the same. These relationships function to stabilize us and keep us grounded in what we find important.

Our anchors can come and go; stability and constant relationships aren't always permanent, and when we experience big changes in life, our anchors are usually some of the first relationships to feel those shifts. As we grow and expand our hopes and ambitions, these relationships must meet the demands of those shifts, as they risk becoming liabilities, or at the least points of stress. We spend a lot of time and energy invested in our anchors, so when things turn south, not taking matters personally is really hard to do.

People we are anchored to have a direct connection to us. We share a psychic link that grants them almost immediate access to our energy body. If the person on the other end of the line isn't in a good place, whatever vibes they are dealing with can travel right through that connection and make their way to us. This, of course, works both ways, and these lines of connection can be used intentionally to send good vibes, not just the bad.

Permanent anchors, the long-term kind, can honestly be a force for good or a force for evil in our lives. For most of us, they are good and beneficial, we have good parents who love us and friends who help us make it through the hard times. We establish communities and intentional families, and wonderful things blossom from those connections. However, for some of us the people we are related to or are connected to by history or blood are harmful influences who can really make life difficult. I'm fortunate to have both.

I say fortunate because all of these connections have served to help me understand who I am and what the world is. We all have to figure that sort of stuff out on our own, but I think our true self really comes to the surface in how we choose to love other people. Nothing tests that like our anchors.

We can love someone and not love the energy they create. We can love someone and not love their toxic or destructive behavior. We can love someone who is not capable of loving us back. We can love someone who hurt us. What we must never do (especially as spiritually sensitive people) is hold space for them to create more chaos or pain.

As we move through the rest of the chapter, keep in mind that you may be intimately connected to someone who is creating problems for you mentally, spiritually, or even physically. If you want the problem to stop, this will likely mean cutting that person out for a while until you are both in a different place, or longer.

ETHERIC CORDS

The psychic link that connects us to our anchors is referred to as an *etheric cord*, otherwise known as an etheric tether or a silver cord. We don't just send psychic energy down them; they respond to our thoughts and movements as well. They are the reason we intuitively know when people we love need us or maybe are lying to us, and for those random tugs we get from people in our past.

Cords eventually fade, become fragile, and break if they aren't maintained and fed a fresh supply of energy. If you are tuned in enough, you'll feel that break in the form of nostalgic thinking or flashes of memories you'd long forgotten. Suddenly, you'll remember a childhood friend that you'd been close with over a summer but hadn't talked to since. It took a while, but eventually the psychic link you shared fizzled out. You'll always remember them, but you're no longer linked; they might as well be a character in a book.

As you might imagine, it isn't just anchors we have these connections with—we actually develop them with anyone we become friends with, anyone who sees the real us, or who we let in. On a psychic level, when we break up with a partner or a friend, part of what makes the whole thing so difficult is that the cord gets ripped, and we feel that wound spiritually.

We can also develop these connections to places, objects, and animals. Basically, anything you can develop an emotional connection to gets an etheric tether.

EXERCISE FOURTEEN
Cord Cutting

Cord cutting is a form of psychic surgery that is done to sever the etheric connection between two people. It can also be done on places and things, and even as a treatment method for relieving addictions. This exercise is done on connections that we are aware of and likely have history with.

The act is simple, but the overall process is difficult because once the connection has been cut intentionally, we have to do everything in our power to stay away from whatever or whoever it is that we just cut out. Meaning, we can't do a cord cutting on a former friend we are going to see every week at church or on an ex-husband who we share custody arrangements with. This is not something we do as a matter of wishful thinking but rather as a last resort when that connection turns toxic.

Once the connection is severed, the person or energy on the opposite end is likely to feel it and may attempt to reestablish the connection. Take this as a sign that it worked, but remain vigilant not to bring them in. It is okay to be civil as you seek closure if necessary, but keep in mind that during these moments we are susceptible to potentially undoing our work. After a cord cutting, I recommend a thorough personal cleansing be done and protections increased.

To do this, perform part one of the Lasers! Exercise in chapter 1. Visualize the other person (or object, vice, place) on the opposite side of an empty room and a silver, iridescent cord that tethers you. At this time, I like to "sterilize with gratitude," wherein I send gratitude for all lessons learned from this connection down the cord. It is both a way of acknowledging the end and a way to prepare my energy body for what comes next.

Visualize beams of liquid light emitting from your hands and targeting the cord, roughly three feet in front of you at the same location. Take it slow, follow your intuition, and let the energy cut through the connection. This could take a few seconds to a few minutes. At this time, I like to say a few words to myself about why I'm releasing the connection and reaffirm my commitment to putting as much distance as I can between myself and that person. When finished, take a salt bath.

BAD APPLES

There are folks out there who have bad vibes that runneth over into everything and every part of their lives. For whatever reason, they keep themselves stuck in a dark place and bring everyone who gets close to them into the darkness. They are predators, intentionally or unintentionally seeking out people to control and manipulate. Life is about them, and they are the only ones who matter. Empathy exists as a one-way street, and all roads lead to them. One might use the term *narcissistic* to summarize their personalities.

Bad apples have a habit of finding spiritually open and sensitive people to manipulate. It's like watching a snake unhinge its jaw and swallow a light bulb. Whatever brilliant light that was shining is now slithering off in the belly of a beast and the world gets a little darker with each second. I've been one of those light bulbs and chances are you have been too.

Over the years, I have had to do a lot of personal work around this because I am a sucker for a good comeback, and I've eagerly held space for bad apples in hopes of helping them heal. Healing happens every day, but you have to want it and then you have to do the things necessary to make it happen. It is easier to take the healing others are doing and masquerade it as your own, however. That's what bad apples tend to do.

Bad apples tend to be big personalities and have big personal orbits. Spiritually sensitive people can become immersed in the vibrations these people put out and sometimes these vibes can be intoxicating or downright addicting. Let's take a closer look at three tactics bad apples use to prey upon spiritually sensitive people.

THE TWIN FLAME CONSPIRACY

The concept of twin flames is a really beautiful one. It's this belief that there are people in the world who share the same spark as you, the same thing that makes you special is also somehow inside of them, and that means your connection to them is rooted in something special. Soul mates and twin flames are essentially the same thing, the term *soul mate* being primarily used to describe romantic partnerships and *twin flame* being someone unromantic, such as a friend, a family member, a mentor, or even a coworker, though twin flame bonds can be romantic.

It's difficult to trace the origins of where this concept came from, but it is believed by some that it came from Plato's *Symposium*. In it, he describes protohumans as having four arms and two faces, which frightened the gods so they split us apart and cursed us to wander the earth looking for our other half. What was likely a romantic myth that explained why we long for connection is twisted into one that tells us we are not whole without someone else. On one hand, that has a sort of tragic beauty to it, but on the other it is downright abusive.

To the spiritually minded, the notion that there is a connection that was made just for us is like finding gold. If you value spiritual growth and exploration, promises of finding someone else who understands you so deeply can be the single deciding factor in what direction we head in life. We all want to be whole, and we all want to feel loved and needed, and this is something that bad apples prey on.

This notion of twin flames glares in the face of most spiritual teachings, which stress that we are each whole and part of the whole. I can't begin to tell you how many times I've had to talk a distraught lover down after a breakup with someone they believed to be their twin flame. The idea that they found their one person and that they might have missed their chance can be devastating.

Twin flame is not a role, it's a classification. We have many twin flames, and if we are lucky, we will meet them. The only true way of knowing if the person is really a twin flame is to see if they add to your light, not diminish it. They will lift you up and trust you, not tear you down and doubt you.

PAST-LIFE PROMISES

This is the same kind of idea. Bad apples use unverifiable spiritual information to bamboozle the spiritually open, and there is nothing quite so seductive as the concept of shared past lives. I fell for this one myself, and the whole experience put me off working on my past lives for many years.

Like we discussed in the previous chapter, our past lives can absolutely have an effect on this lifetime. Promises and agreements we've made in previous lives can haunt us in the next, but they are just shadows of something we used to be.

My general rule of thumb is that if a court of law would throw out a legal agreement signed when someone was drunk, then whatever I agreed to do in a past life should be thrown out as well. I don't know the state I was in or the circumstances that led me to it, and I certainly am not the same person. Just because you might share a past life with someone doesn't mean you have to share this one with them. Sometimes things are better left where they started. At the very least, you get to decide if you want to continue those agreements in this life.

GAINFUL GURU

The last tactic that I want to discuss is what I call *gainful gurus*. These are spiritual teachers or advisors who abuse their spiritual authority at the cost of their followers' peace of mind, financial security, or happiness. These relationships can be difficult to spot until you are in too deep. Once spotted, they can be difficult to break away from for a myriad of reasons. Our spiritual teachers have a lot of sway over us and it's hard to confront that once you suspect something is wrong.

I charge for classes I teach and for roughly half of the services I offer. I understand the importance of being able to pay the bills, and I don't think what I do is any less important than what a minister does, so why shouldn't I get paid for it? The judgment I'm suggesting we make is not in the making of money for work, it is in understanding how and when it can be predatory.

If a teacher ever tries to hold your spiritual salvation, fate, or afterlife hostage until you behave a certain way, pay a certain amount of money, or allow/excuse inappropriate behavior; they are a bad apple. No one has that type of authority over you.

It is easy for bad apples to work their way into our lives and assume the position of an anchor. Not all bad apples try to spoil the rest of us intentionally, and whatever it is that has led them to being agents of predation is surely something we shouldn't wish on anyone. We still need to be weary of them and their splash radius so we can mitigate their influence.

GROUPS AND COMMUNITIES

Being social creatures, it is natural for us to want to belong and be part of something bigger. Forming bonds with groups of people and communities can be a beautiful thing that provides security and a place to belong. When those groups turn on us or decide we are no longer welcome, all that love and support can quickly turn into malice and resentment. Now instead of dealing with the bad vibes of one person, you have multiple people jumping on the bandwagon and the problems grow exponentially.

It should be said that a lot of us have to work or go to school, and we can't simply avoid the social factor. Each of the unique types of bad vibes we talk about here, and in other chapters, can (and likely will) be part of daily life for many of us. We can encounter another person's bad vibes anywhere people gather, and this is especially true of people and places we interact with frequently.

All of the tactics and problems we've discussed in the first few chapters can each make themselves present in these situations and, if the group is strong enough, you have to deal with their *collective consciousness*, their group-mind. This collective consciousness creates its own frequency, which only serves to reinvigorate the bad vibes everyone is feeling. It's essentially a personification of mob mentality.

Not all collective consciousnesses are bad or should be avoided, nor can we necessarily avoid them with any degree of ease. What makes collective consciousnesses scary is that wherever they place their focus, large amounts of energy are sure to follow. If that energy is negative, then that collective consciousness might as well be a weapon of mass destruction.

On the other hand, we also run the risk of joining a community and then taking on the bad qualities they possess without being aware it is happening. In our search to fit in, we eagerly make connections with others, and that gives them, and their vibe, a place in our lives. This goes the same for whatever collective consciousness we become part of. Once we start to identify with parts of the group, we are already assimilating the group's vibration into our own.

STRANGE VIBES

Alright, so up to this point we've been focused on the psychic energies that we as individuals create and can pass on to one another. We talked about how it happens and why it happens, but it's all been relatively common, natural stuff. It's normal for us to run into bad apples and to join groups only to find out we aren't a good fit, then deal with the energetic ramifications of that experience. It isn't normal for energy to be malicious or for it to be intentionally dangerous.

Let's take a look at other types of energy that we might come in contact with from others that have a bit more of a bite.

« RUDE ENERGY »
Disturbance Level: 1

Rude energy is exactly what it sounds like. It is energy that collects and manifests as vibrations that we find offensive. Rude energy isn't necessarily bad; it is just not for us and therefore makes us feel unwelcome. What is rude to us may not be rude to other people. Rude energy usually develops as a result of miscommunication or misunderstanding, but that doesn't mean it's harmless. It can make us angry, violent, depressed, and a whole host of ugly things that we typically aren't embodying. It can also trigger our fight-or-flight reflexes.

Usually, this type of energy is a first-impression type of thing and is based on preconceived notions or ignorance. Like any vibe we take personally, rude energy can follow us around for a long time after we interact with it.

« THE EVIL EYE »
Disturbance Level: 1

The evil eye is an unintentional curse placed on a person, a place, or a thing that is caused by jealousy. We say unintentional because the majority of the time the evil eye is passed without the caster's consent.

Anyone, regardless of how pure their soul, can cast it. Intention has nothing to do with this type of bad vibe; that's what makes it so dangerous. Even our closest friends and family can be the ones to give it to us.

Evil eyes manifest in various ways, but a sure tell that something is under attack by one is that it was coveted by others and then begins to deteriorate. This can be relationships, physical goods or objects, business deals, or anything.

The evil eye is very much like fungus: it only takes a spore to settle onto something, and if the conditions are right, a whole colony of bad vibes has appeared within a matter of a few days. If we don't take care of it, then it will spread and potentially destroy whatever it was consuming.

When you get a new house, a new job, a new car, a new relationship, a new child, or do any leveling up in life, people are going to take it personally. We can't help but to compare ourselves to others, and that causes a ridiculous amount of low-level psychic disturbances that ultimately culminate in something like the evil eye.

We should be particularly aware of the evil eye when it comes to matters of success or career. Of all the spaces we are likely to run into a bad vibration like the evil eye, the workplace is high on the list. This is especially true after a promotion or recognition. So many of us draw our identities from our careers, and when we feel we aren't adding up, or that we deserved something someone else got, we can easily pass the evil eye along.

People who are spiritually gifted are particularly vulnerable to being evil eye casters. Jealousy is a strong emotion, and it can creep up on us from time to time. To keep yourself from doing this accidentally, whenever you find yourself getting jealous or feeling awkward about someone else's success, say this little mantra:

> It is their time for this; my time will come.
> Being happy for them paves a path for
> my own aspirations to manifest.

« CURSES (INTENTIONAL) »
Disturbance Level: 2–5

Curses are a very real phenomena that happen, and while I think people tend to jump to the worst possible scenario too easily, they are something we should be wary of. Curses are intentional psychic/spiritual energy that is sent for malicious purposes.

Curses are meant to harm us, restrict us, and/or to take away our free will. I'm mature enough to know that sometimes these things can be used for good and that everything in the spiritual world contains nuance. I am also wise enough to know that if someone is resorting to curses, then there is something wrong with them. Healthy, happy, well-adjusted people don't curse others. If someone is spending the time and resources to go out of their way to hurt someone, then it is a safe bet that there is a lot more going on than we are aware of.

I've been battling curses for most of my professional life; it is one of the most common concerns for people when they seek me out. Sometimes their worry is valid, but most of the time when someone thinks they are cursed their predicament is caused by something much less malicious. When the issue is a curse, however, understanding how they develop and get their power is key to combating them.

There are small curses that, like the evil eye, are not meant to be big deals. They are mean or hateful thoughts said and sent in a heated moment that we don't really intend to send. Most of the curses out there are these, and they don't really hold a candle to the more extreme variety.

The real power in a larger curse is in the potency of belief around it. The caster can go through any number of practices to drum up negative energy. This can be anything from summoning spirits to inflicting pain on someone to funneling the resulting energy into the working. Sometimes curses are just writing your name on a piece of paper and spitting on it before throwing it in a fire, and sometimes the caster goes to extremes to meet their ends. All of this is done to create energy that can be sent (usually) in one shot or magickal act. Once that energy is sent, it latches on, and in order for it to stick and do its thing, it has to wiggle its way into your life and set up shop. The more fearful you are of a curse, the more energy you give it.

Usually, the effects will pass over you if you can weather the initial attack without getting involved or engaging the energy. If, however, you are receptive to the energy during the initial process, then the curse has an easy way in. To ensure this, those who curse us usually do something to get our attention to let us know we are under attack. They might leave remnants of the working on our doorstep or even taunt us online. None of this is necessary; it only serves to make the initial attack more likely to succeed. If we don't respond or engage, the curse has a much harder time infiltrating our lives.

Even if you don't engage it, the energy is still going to hang around you and continue to look for a way in until it is too weak to continue.

Generational curses are passed down from generation to generation in a family. They are deeply embedded in the spiritual psyche of the family and are the most difficult to break because often we are not sure where they came from, only their effects. While generational curses can be those cast by a nonfamily member onto the family line, most often they are cast unintentionally by a family member who precedes us.

They are also unlike other curses in that they usually construct themselves around a specific area of family life and often trap decedents in a pattern of belief or behavior. For example, if your great-great-grandparents murdered someone for money and the family wealth comes as a result, the family wealth could easily be cursed. If there is a history of abuse and neglect in your family, chances are that it is related to some sort of generational curse.

Generational curses latch on and create conditions that are difficult to escape. Tackling them can be difficult and complex, and it must include counseling or therapy, as often this type of curse involves trauma. Unless the current members of the family who are afflicted deal with the current trauma surrounding the curse, the curse will continue to remain linked to the family.

« PSYCHIC VAMPIRES »
Disturbance Level: 2

One of the most misunderstood groups of people on the planet are those who fall into the category of psychic vampires. Psychic vampires are people who feed off of the vital energy produced by other people. After interacting with them, we usually feel drained or tired, we might get depressed, and over time this can turn into a very big issue for some. While most psychic vampires are completely unaware that they do this, a very small few do it intentionally. Generally in these instances, the person they are feeding from is a willing participant in the exchange. It is said to produce a state of ecstasy or euphoria when done right.

Psychic vampirism is a form of psychic ability, and those who are psychically sensitive are likely to have some degree of this trait in the mix. The ability turns on as a survival mechanism when vital energy is low; we naturally replenish ourselves with ambient spiritual energy, which just happens to come off in spades from other people. Does that make us monsters? No, not at all.

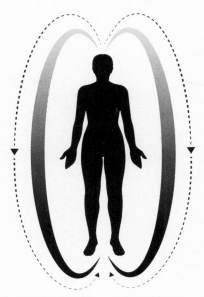

OUR AURIC FIELD AND ENERGY BODIES

For people who have vampirism as their main ability, the stigma surrounding the process can keep them from understanding how they work as psychic beings. Psychic vampires make incredibly powerful mediums and channelers, and most learn to draw life force from non-human or nonliving objects.

There is also a small group of people who get labeled as psychic vampires but aren't, instead of feeding from our life force, they accidentally collect it. We like to think of our energy bodies as flowing upward through the body and exiting through the top of the head. The energy then gets reabsorbed at the feet, creating something that looks a bit like a water fountain shooting energy upward and falling down into a basin (see illustration above). This energy that is moving in and out of the body produces the auric field.

For most of us, this model fits, but it's not the same for everyone; there are people whose energy runs the opposite direction and people whose energy runs outward from their solar plexus. The torus is still there, it just has a different point of origin and a different flow. This means that interactions with these people are going to feel awkward, and our energy is likely to get caught up in theirs.

My main concern with psychic vampires is in remembering that they are humans too. They likely don't know they are doing it, and to demonize them is not only unfair but silly. That doesn't mean we have to be at their whim or let anyone take our energy without consent; it just means we should approach these people with the same degree of compassion that we would hope to receive.

The psychic cleansing and protection work we will do in chapters 7 and 8 should be more than capable of handling unwanted psychic vampirism. Just because someone might not do it intentionally, doesn't mean you have to be on the receiving end. We can have empathy and boundaries at the same time.

As a general rule, it is always a good idea to ground and center your energy body as we discussed previously if you feel like you've been fed from. This simple act will reboot your energy centers and get vital energies moving again. It also isn't a bad idea to eat something with protein and to channel Source energy through the center of your body, allowing it to drain off into the earth below. Both eating and using Source energy will help replenish your vital energies quickly.

CONCLUSION AND JOURNALING

In this chapter, we discussed how, like ourselves, other people can be messy with how they use their vital energies. We talked about how sometimes that energy can become a problem in shared spaces and how interactions with other people and their energy can affect our vibration. In the next chapter, we are going to jump into environments and locations, as well as the preternatural vibrations and frequencies that are associated with them.

We talked about a lot in this chapter and things got a little weird, as promised. Respond to the following journaling prompts to the best of your ability to help clarify how this information directly relates to you.

1. Who are the people in your life who fulfill the function of anchor for you? Do you feel positively about these relationships? If not, in what ways are these anchors a problem for your vital energies? What about them should be adjusted so that your connection is balanced?

2. Rude energy is something that we run into a lot. What are instances where you've encountered it and where was the energy coming from? Was it situational or personal?

3. The evil eye is one of the most common forms of curse out there. Have you had an experience with it personally? If so, how did you deal with the situation and what would you do different now after reading the chapter?

4. Have you been on the receiving end of an intentional curse in the past? How did you resolve it?

5. If you have had an experience with psychic vampirism, describe how it felt on a physical, spiritual, and mental level and what the recovery process looked like.

5

ENVIRONMENTAL AND PRETERNATURAL BAD VIBES

If you thought things got weird in the previous chapter, this one is going to be a doozy! As we continue our exploration of bad vibrations, we now move into the territory of what is considered to be nightmare fuel for many. My goal here isn't to freak you out or to add fuel to any stress you might be experiencing, but rather to shed light on some of the most extreme psychic/spiritual activity that we can encounter.

Those who are afflicted by the preternatural will find answers here and those who are new to the world of the psychic and spiritual will discover a lot of useful information that I wish I'd had when I began my journey. The sage psychic, especially mediums, will find detail information about specific types of spirits and activity that are known to be difficult to discern and deal with.

Most of the issues we experience related to land and physical locations fall under the category of the preternatural, which we will also dive into in this chapter. When discussing these matters, location and environment are often linked to whatever is the cause of the preternatural disturbance. Separating the two felt unnecessary and like it might complicate our work.

Vibes accumulate over time and become part of their location just like they can become part of us. Sometimes these vibes are the result of things we've done and sometimes their cause is rooted in matters far older and much greater than us. Physical locations generate their own form of spiritual energy and in some instances that energy can coalesce into something intelligent, all without the need for us to be involved. Some, myself included, believe that it is this process that filled the primordial world with the spirits that our ancestors called gods.

OUR HOMES

Home is where the heart is, they say. I like to think that is true, but either way it is a great metaphor for how homes collect their psychic energy. Our homes are directly tied to our identities; we paint them, we decorate, and we line the halls with photos depicting family and friends. Inside them, we experience everything from love to rage and that makes them the perfect receptacle for our psychic energy and our psychic waste.

Psychic waste is the residual and excess psychic energy that can build up over time in a place. It serves no purpose, and too much of it can cause spiritual health issues. We slough off this energy like dead skin cells when we are feeling relaxed and when sleeping. It's just part of our natural energy cycle.

The way to combat buildup is by keeping energy moving and by doing regular cleansings, but homes still tend to hold on to vibrations more than other locations. Psychic waste is usually carried out naturally when energy moves throughout the home but easily gets stuck. I maintain good flow by opening up windows and removing as much clutter as possible, whenever possible. Fumigation (i.e., the burning of herbs and resins), which we will talk about in the next chapter, is another good option.

This could be because of the way they are constructed. Most homes have spaces where energy is blocked and unable to move in or out. In

feng shui, these are called *chi traps*. It is common for apartment buildings to have chi traps between units and for them to be unintentionally
created by decor. The general rule of thumb is that airflow is key; if
you find a place where air isn't moving freely, chances are it's trapping
energy.

WORK AND SCHOOL

At work and school, we don't necessarily have psychic waste buildup
as a major concern but we still have to worry about the intentional and
unintentional psychic energy that is flinging around from other people. Don't get me wrong, these places still have energy traps, but it's
rare that they pose a large threat because these locations still see a lot
of movement.

Work and schools are susceptible to the formation of psychic fields
of energy caused by the group-mind or a collective consciousness.
These locations are also likely to house rude energy. Cleansing these
locations is difficult, so it is usually best to cleanse yourself after and to
protect before and during exposure.

ONLINE

Something that is becoming more apparent with each year is that the
internet is very much alive, at least in the spiritual sense. There are many
who believe that algorithms are like spirits and can even be petitioned
to help with getting likes and followers. It makes sense, as it's all just
information and energy at the end of the day, and how else would we
define a spirit when it all boils down?

While I can't verify the internet's personhood, I can say from my
experience that it does have psychic/spiritual properties that are similar
to those of a physical location. When online, even when doing so from

the comfort of your own home, you are entering a space where people meet, where goods and information are exchanged, and where we can even display our art and explore our interests. We are vulnerable to the same type of frequencies and vibrations that we would be if we were entering a public square. It is even worse in some ways because we are also engaging that location from a place of comfort (your home or your phone), making us more susceptible to the rogue energy found therein.

Aside from doing regular psychic/spiritual hygiene to keep online energies from seeping into your life, another excellent way to do this is to clear your browser's cached data. Your machine literally stores online information as a means of making it easier to access later, which means there are pieces of the internet *and* its vibes that are probably on your personal computer right now.

LAND AND LEY LINES

Our planet is incredible and has this energy thing completely figured out. Like us, the earth has veins and arteries that move vital energies throughout its body, which we refer to as ley lines. Ley lines are natural channels that attract spirits, spiritual energy, and psychic phenomena. Most ley lines we interact with on the surface are positive or at least benign by our standards, and we hardly notice them. Usually, it takes someone who is spiritually plugged in or naturally psychic to discover them, though they are easily found by dowsing.

Some ley lines bring "positive" energy from deep within the core while others take the "negative" back for transmutation. What is positive or negative in this sense is incredibly nuanced, but we do know that most of the exposed ley lines that have been mapped generally feel like positive places to visit. However, some of them feel negative and develop reputations for being cursed or haunted land. One such ley line is said to run through Salem, Massachusetts; another is said to run right through the plains of the continental United States—both of which I have experienced and both of which left me with a strong psychic impression.

If your home or a location you visit is located on or near one of these lines, you are likely to experience heightened psychic phenomena and spiritual activity as a general rule of thumb. They not only attract spirits and spiritual energies but also amplify psychic ability and may be a contributing factor in cases where poltergeists are present.

Cities tend to be built on top of ley lines, and this isn't necessarily a spiritual coincidence. Ley lines are often found running with streams, rivers, and underground wells, all of which are essential to city planning. If you live in a highly populated area, find a local map and look at how the area has been laid out and planned. You can also look online for a map of ley lines, but I usually find these to be missing a lot of the smaller tributaries.

« VORTICES »
Disturbance Level: 4

A vortex is a bridge that connects our plane to other planes of being, and it is a strange and exciting phenomenon to explore. It is neither good nor bad; however, the effect on its surrounding environment can be a nightmare for those who encounter one.

The best way to explain a vortex is to think of it like a tornado; it develops as a result of multiple forms of atmospheric energy converging at just the right time, with just the right conditions present. Normally, these energies move around each other, but because the conditions are just right, they end up crashing into and altering the direction of each other's current. Inside the space where they interact, an energetic funnel forms, which is the start of a vortex.

Over time, with enough (and the right kind of) collected energy in that location, the vortex will continue to grow and, eventually, can become so strong that it stabilizes on our plane, becoming a semipermanent fixture. Vortices will often open and close at will, depending on conditions such as time of day, the season, and even weather.

The most difficult thing about a vortex is that we cannot control where it ultimately opens to when it develops naturally. Stable vortices are mappable and predictable in this manner, but those that aren't stable can easily shift between multiple planes without a discernible pattern.

Though rare, vortices can develop in any location, especially if those who frequent it are spiritually minded. By tapping into Source near a potential vortex, we inadvertently end up opening it wider and potentially even programming it. If this is all done unintentionally through rogue psychic energy, the results can be chaotic.

Vortices seem like a natural place to jump into what I like to call, the preternatural.

PRETERNATURAL BAD VIBES

Preternatural is my preferred term for what is often referred to as the supernatural or paranormal. The latter two words suggest an unnatural occurrence, whereas preternatural is defined as something that is natural but extraordinary and simply unexplainable with our current understanding. It expands to include the psychic, spiritual, extraterrestrial, and even cryptid.

As I mentioned earlier, preternatural activity is often linked to a location, as many of the beings or phenomena we will discuss are usually location based. This won't always be the case, and I will make sure to mention when it isn't, but as a general rule of thumb we often see things like hauntings and elementals as being related to one location.

« ATTACHMENTS »
Disturbance Level: 3–5

Attachments are spirits and other forms of energy that cling to us. Sometimes this is by happenstance and are temporary, other times these are intentional and long term. Attachments aren't necessarily bad; spirit guides are a type of attachment, but they can be a problem if not welcome. Attachments aren't necessarily feeding off of you either—they could just be along for a ride and you are simply their mode of transport from one location to the next. The danger comes when an uninvited attachment develops a parasitic relationship with its host.

Parasitic relationships come in all sizes, from acute to raging, so it is best to know what you should be looking for. The first thing to remember is that parasitic spirits aren't necessarily demonic, in fact, most of them aren't. The majority of those attracted to humans were human or at least originated from humans in the first place. Since I mentioned the D word, let's go ahead and dive in.

« DEMONS (PARASITIC) »
Disturbance Level: 3–5

Demons are real; they just aren't what you probably have been led to believe they are. This is in part due to the term being used to describe many different types of spirits over time. In fact, most of us are raised to believe that any spirit that isn't of the "one true god" is a demonic force. By this rationale, that means even the Buddha is a demon, and I just can't get behind that line of reasoning.

We even have a word, *demonize*, which means "to portray as wicked or bad." In a world where anything can be demonized, it is hard to pinpoint a distinct culprit, which I think has led to an overabundant use of the word. This is especially true in the world of preternatural study where the word is thrown around and used to label any spirit that isn't docile. The spiritual world, however, is not docile, nor are those who reside therein. For our purposes, let us whittle down this definition to something that is tangible and useful for battling bad vibes.

Demons are extremely rare parasitic spirits that subsist on chaos and decay. They are intelligent, calculating, and attach themselves to people by hijacking the psychic connection meant for spirit guides. They manifest slowly and usually are drawn to those with a strong emotional and/or psychic sensitivity. They attach themselves during times of extreme stress and gently wiggle their way into the mind, body, and spirit. Most demonic attacks are short lived and go unnoticed, but on occasion they find a host that is ideal for long-term grooming.

Demonic grooming involves preparing a host for an extended period of feeding that, if undisturbed, generally leads to involuntary possession and ultimately death. While legitimate demonic possession can be a possibility, this is an incredibly rare occurrence and is not one that should be treated alone, nor will it be treatable with only one application.

Parasitic demons can be difficult to tackle for many reasons, the least of which is that there is a ton of baggage that comes along with the concept of possession. It's also difficult in that symptoms such as overshadowing, which will develop as part of the parasitic relationship, can often look like mental instability. There is a fine line between the two, and in my personal view, there are many things that connect mental instability and spiritual parasitism. I'm not saying one guarantees the other, but I am saying that demonic parasitism often leads to mental instability as a means of breaking down the host.

In these extreme cases of involuntary possession, the damage that is caused by the infestation is life-altering and remains with the afflicted in some form or another throughout their lifetimes. I have never heard of someone walking away from a full-on involuntary possession without suffering from the related trauma. These are people who have had their willpower taken from them and who were made to experience extreme mental, spiritual, and even physical abuse at the compulsion of their parasite. That isn't something that someone can easily come back from, especially when most people don't take this issue seriously.

The movies do get a few things right when it comes to demons. For instance, demons have a handful of vulnerabilities that can be exploited. The first is that holy water works, but it has to be used by someone with a high level of faith in the power of that holy water. I have seen nonbelievers use it with no effect, but devout Catholics use it with incredible results. The next is that religious iconography does agitate the parasite, regardless of what culture we come from. What seems to matter most is the religious background or leanings of the afflicted. As long as those symbols activate their spiritual and mental centers in a positive way, they get the job done.

What the movies get wrong is that demons aren't all in league with the devil. There is a hierarchy of demonic spirits that some religious groups and spiritual traditions recognize, but those are more like minor deities than parasites. Getting the name of a spirit, any spirit, does give you an amount of control over their influence, including demons. However, parasitic demons aren't often the famous kind and discovering their name can be incredibly difficult for even the most talented of mediums.

« INCUBI/SUCCUBI »
Disturbance Level: 4–5

This is a classification of spirit that is particularly known for attachments and throughout history has appeared in various forms. They are often considered to be demons, depending on tradition. It is my understanding from personal observation that these aren't two different kinds of being but rather one form that appears as masculine, feminine, or neither, depending on the sexual appetite of its victim. An incubus can move from one person to the next in a household regardless of their gender; sexuality and sexual preference are merely the tools that it uses to achieve its goals.

Sexual energy is a direct link to our life force, and in many cultures, they are considered one and the same. Incubi attach themselves to us and use our (usually repressed) sexual desires to activate this energy and siphon it. Once they are attached, the person experiences a change in their libido or can begin to establish performance issues in the bedroom, including a lack of interest or erectile dysfunction. After they have taken all the available energy, usually at the cost of destroying their victim's sex life, they move on to the next person.

« *ELEMENTALS AND FAERIES* »
Disturbance Level: 2–5
This is a term that gets used in different ways to describe different beings. From an esoteric perspective, elementals are spiritual distillations of elemental power and usually avoid humans like the plague. We wouldn't find one of them randomly hanging out on our plane of existence, and we usually have to go to great lengths to communicate with them. In the world of paranormal reality television, the term elemental is often used as a placeholder for what would traditionally be referred to as a *faery (fairy, fae).*

The distinction is subtle, I suppose, but faeries are more likely to interact with humans, especially if we set up shop near them. In some areas, entire religions have been devoted to them. They interact with us like ghosts would, though usually more mischievously, and make themselves known through pranks, sabotage, and even by mimicking other spirits all in order to get our attention.

Attachments are highly unlikely with elementals and faeries; they tend to look down on us or at least do not trust us. Humans lie, murder, steal, and do all sorts of things that they'd rather not get involved in. When they do, usually they use our own tactics against us, which makes them unreliable and untrustworthy.

« ETHERIC WILDLIFE »
Disturbance Level: 1–5

The spiritual world is a reflection of our own, and just as we have animals and insects that are part of a great cycle on our plane, other planes share a similar setup. *Etheric wildlife* is a term used to describe the myriad of (mostly) minor spiritual entities from the other planes of being who meander over to our side of the fence from time to time. They come in all shapes and sizes and often go unnoticed by those who haven't embraced their psychic abilities because they tend to blend right into their environments.

They feed off of residual psychic energy, so you are likely to find them in abandoned buildings or in haunted locations, though they are not ghosts or spirits in the traditional Western sense. They appear to me as large insects, sometimes mounded into groups that cluster in dark corners and in unused closets. They aren't dangerous or pose any sort of threat, they are docile toward the living and are more afraid of us than we are of them. They don't communicate with us, they just linger and feed, like wood lice, devouring psychic debris and left over imprints.

If they are present in a location, the likelihood of a haunting is higher, though their presence doesn't necessarily indicate a haunting. They are also drawn to poltergeists as well as places such as landfills and cemeteries. That said, they are drawn to locations where energy has become stagnant, and usually those places also have other types of activity.

A true study of etheric wildlife would reveal a lot of crossover with elementals and ghosts. A key difference is that etheric wildlife won't be able to communicate with us the same way a ghost or an elemental can.

« GHOSTS »
Disturbance Level: 3–5

Ghosts are earthbound spirits that get stuck here for any number of reasons. Most of the time, ghosts are harmless, going about their business, not necessarily even aware of us. Ghosts tend to get tunnel vision, becoming fixated on a certain person, place, or thing, which brings us to the territory of hauntings. While hauntings can produce harmful phenomena and there are ghosts that can be dangerous for us to interact with, most ghosts are harmless if not helpful. An important thing to remember is that they are still human beings having a human experience; approaching ghosts with empathy is always a good idea.

We are most likely to encounter what are often referred to as *residual hauntings,* which are caused by residual ghosts/spirits/psychic impressions. These occur when psychic/spiritual energy is imprinted onto an area or an item and is more like a movie clip than an intelligent spirit. Residual hauntings are basically tiny psychic pieces of a person that got stuck somewhere and now play on loop or that respond to specific sets of stimuli. These are the hauntings that involve hearing footsteps every night at the same time or seeing someone walk through the living room each night at dusk. They are often triggered by timing or by other environmental shifts.

Residual hauntings can be frightening, but they are, by their nature, harmless to us as the remnants of the spirit remain trapped in its own self-isolation. Residual hauntings do attract other forms of spirit, such as etheric wildlife. Usually, residual hauntings are one of multiple issues happening at a location. This style of haunting is caused by similar phenomena to poltergeists, and the two can sometimes be difficult to differentiate.

Traditional ghosts are the second most common and are responsible for what we call *traditional hauntings*. There is a wide range of potential here for how the spirit manifests and what they are interested in. Typically they are invested in a person, a place, or a thing and are intelligent. By this, I mean that it is possible to communicate with them and carry on entire conversations. Sometimes they are loved ones checking in and sometimes they are previous owners, or potentially someone who even died in the home. The common misconception with traditional ghosts is that they need our help to cross over and that they have unfinished business. This just simply isn't true. The majority of traditional ghosts are just people who have decided not to move on and quite enjoy hanging out in the ether.

Ideally, a mutually beneficial relationship can be established with traditional ghosts. Many people have learned to live with a spectral roommate. To ensure that the ghost is a ghost and not something else, communicate as much with the spirit as you can, as frequently as you can, and get whatever meaningful details you can about their physical life. Often, if someone passed away in a location there is record of that. Matching historical references to the information you get from the spirit is the best way to ensure you are speaking to an authentic traditional ghost. Calling in a medium if that is not your specific skill set is also a great way to get details about the spirit.

Hungry ghosts are spirits that remain here out of an extreme emotional need that causes them to be violent and animalistic. They are essentially the psychic energy of the body that goes unguided by the mind or spirit and are in many ways rogue predators. Hungry ghosts attach themselves to people and drain their life force and emotional energy before moving on to another host. Hungry ghosts can easily, over time, become demonic parasites. Regular spiritual hygiene will sever the connection between the spirit and the afflicted, especially if caught early on.

HAUNTED OBJECTS

In the same way that a location can be haunted, a physical item can be as well. There are, however, some noticeable differences between the two. Rarely is a traditional or a hungry ghost associated with a haunted object; however, we do see a higher number of cases where objects have residual-style hauntings. This lends itself to the notion that haunted objects aren't necessarily haunted by spirits in the usual sense, but rather by psychic imprints and thoughtforms. Only in the rarest of cases is there an intelligent spirit attached to an item.

In haunted item cases, the residual phenomena is usually triggered by an emotional attachment to the item or a moment of psychic/spiritual distress. The energies involved in these hauntings often respond to our needs and wants and, depending on the item, have the ability to grow exponentially. For instance, a doll that is haunted and passed on to a new child will have no problem finding energy if that child gives it attention. The more we touch, hold, or play with the item, the more energy is transferred to it.

« LAND SPIRITS »
Disturbance Level: 1–5

Land spirits are the spiritual personification of a regional environment. They are the spirits of mountains, valleys, lakes, streams, ravines, forests, and so on. Their relationship to humanity depends on where they are and, like people, no two are the same. There is a lot of mystery and beauty to this subject; however, they are not usually responsible for bad vibes unless they are being mistreated. Usually, land spirits are peaceful and focused, they are something we have to seek out. If, however, the land from which they originate is under attack, they will respond in turn.

Land spirits and elementals differ in that land spirits are much less communicative with us and their energy emanates specifically from one region or location.

« THOUGHTFORMS AND EGREGORES »
Disturbance Level: 1–5

Thoughtforms are psychic intelligences that originate from thoughts, hence the name. That is an oversimplification, of course, but if you remember nothing else, let it be that. The concept of a thoughtform is actually quite heady, but their existence is real and palpable, and they are a frequent problem for those of us in the world of the paranormal and preternatural.

The jury is still out on if thoughtforms are spirits or something else entirely, but almost everyone agrees that they mimic the behavior of spirits. The differences are often so subtle that even experienced mediums can confuse the two. This is an easy and honest mistake, and the only real way to tell the difference between them is to poke them and see if they try to take a bite. Just kidding, mostly.

To understand what a thoughtform is and how to combat it, we need to think like a computer. Just hear me out, I know this is a weird metaphor, but it is going to save us a lot of time. In his paper "Minds, Brains, and Programs," Dr. John Searle presented a thought experiment called "the Chinese Room," and it rocked the minds of the philosophical world (Searle 1980). To summarize, Searle posed the following hypothetical regarding an artificial intelligence that behaved as if it understood (Mandarin) Chinese:

One day, English-speaking programmers are able to create an AI that is capable of understanding Mandarin Chinese. It takes Mandarin characters as input and, through its program, produces other characters, which it provides as output. The program is capable of doing this so convincingly, in fact, that it can fool a native speaker into believing they are communicating with another native speaker regardless of what question they ask.

Searle poses this question to us: Does the program literally understand Mandarin Chinese or is it simulating the ability to understand? He goes on to make several points in his paper and suggests that he could essentially behave as the computer in this situation, given enough time. Even without understanding the output, he could receive Mandarin characters and process them according to a program. He concludes, finally, that without the ability to *understand*, the AI does not have the ability to *think* and therefore does not have a *mind*.

The difference between a spirit and a thoughtform is that thoughtforms are like Chinese Rooms. They look like spirits, smell like spirits, act like spirits, but if you dare to look deep enough you will find that they have a clockwork heart. This makes them more difficult to manage and easy to misdiagnose. Methods for removing spirits will not have the same effect on thoughtforms, often providing temporary relief at best.

Generally speaking, a thoughtform starts off as an idea or a concept, and then it grows through generated belief over time. I remember a case where someone had recently moved into a new condo and believed it was haunted even though none of their neighbors reported any activity and the building was brand new. After much work, it was revealed that the activity didn't start until after a friend (who was particularly fond of believing there were ghosts everywhere) mentioned feeling like they were being watched one night. The client only had to have the thought planted in her mind to make it come alive in her spiritual life. Before long, she was hearing footsteps and feeling like someone was watching her too. She did eventually find relief, but only after wasting money on psychics and exorcists who steered her in the wrong direction.

Egregores are a type of thoughtform that originate from the group-mind of specific individuals. These can be created intentionally, as is done in many esoteric orders, or unintentionally out of a shared belief. Like other thoughtforms, they don't have a mind of their own, but they do tend to share mental space with the group-mind that created it.

So how do you know if you are dealing with a spirit or a thought-form? Ask it a question about you. Spirits, who are intelligent and have a mind of their own, will be able to discern cues from your appearance and vibration, and from the spiritual company you keep. Thought-forms, on the other hand, tend to have one lane they stick to and are not good with changing topics. When communicating with a genuine spirit, they possess a degree of personality that thoughtforms don't, as well. My big go-to is to check in with my spirit guides and have them help assess the situation. When in doubt, ask your guides if you are dealing with a real spirit or an egregore.

The best way, in my experience, to respond to thoughtforms of any kind that manifest as part of a disturbance is to treat the situation as you would any other type of psychic disturbance that isn't a spirit: with a psychic cleansing, not an exorcism. They are particularly vulnerable to the level three "Iron Plug" and "Etheric Stent" exercises that we will discuss in the next part. The key is to not engage them in communication, which we would want to do with a normal spirit. Instead, communicating with them further is only going to help them grow.

« VISITORS »
Disturbance Level: 4–5

The jury is still out on exactly what the visitors are. If we compare modern reports to folklore and recorded history, we see many comparisons to them and faery beings, as well as classical depictions of angels and demons. For most of recent history, we have termed them as *extra-terrestrials* or *aliens;* however, there are many who question whether or not that is technically true. What is evident is that these beings are capable of moving through dimensions that we have always thought were the domain of the spiritual.

We know that visitors are attracted to certain people; that these people claim to be abducted and taken to other locations, usually against their will; and that many of these people report some sort of violation of physical privacy. Sometimes this is known to them during the experience; other times they are only left with a feeling that something had happened. Rarely is there physical evidence, however, and the vast majority of these experiences appear to happen on some form of etheric plane.

Sometimes these experiences are generally peaceful, and the person has a positive exchange. For many, however, the experience is frightening and haunts them their entire lives. Several people report repeated or multiple abductions by visitors over the course of several years.

CONCLUSION AND JOURNALING

In this chapter, we discussed several topics that are often sensational-ized in the media. We peeled back layers of false, and sometimes con-flicting, information to get to the heart of the matter. Now that we have covered everything from past lives to interdimensional visitors, let's take a look at what we can do about them beyond what we have already explored so far.

Respond to the following prompts in your journal and do your best to be as clear as possible with your responses.

1. What is the vibration of your home? Does your home have a supportive feel to it or do you feel drained by it? Why do you think this is?

2. Describe the vibration of your place of work or school. How does that vibration impact you throughout the day? What are areas of your experience there that you'd like to improve through spiritual/psychic means?

3. If you spend a lot of time online, do you find it to be a positive experience or one that causes stress? How do the websites, blogs, and message boards you visit regularly impact your mental and spiritual condition?

4. Have you ever experienced a vortex? If so, describe what it felt like and what spiritual activity you witnessed around it.

5. Parasitic demons are the last thing I think of when I am on a case, but many have sensationalized them, especially on television. What are five other spirits or phenomena that could be to blame for bad vibes that could be mistaken for demonic?

6. Elementals are a part of life, and we can't go far without interacting with them on some level. Describe an experience where you or someone you know came into contact with an elemental.

7. If you were a ghost, how would you want or expect people to communicate with you?

(((PART THREE)))

CLEANSING AND TRIAGE

Spiritual cleansing has been drilled into me through my formal studies in the metaphysical and occult. My teachers have all held the concept of clearing our vital energies of unwanted psychic debris as one of the core principles of a spiritual life. I have, in one form or another, cleansed and purified my energy body, home, car, and office a million times by now and I still don't think I'll ever be done with the job.

I became a true believer in the importance of spiritual cleansing when I started working with clients. Clearing energy became a necessary component of the job and something I found myself doing whenever I made a house call. Eventually, I started offering sessions in my office and it wasn't too long before I met a client that changed my life and the way I understood bad vibes, forever.

To keep a long story short, she had come in with her adult son for a general reading and brought a whole bunch of spirits with her. Initially, I thought the spirits were all trying to come through to bring messages to her, but eventually with the help of my guide, I understood that they were actually trying to get my attention. Specifically, I was being drawn to a part of her energy body near the back of her neck. With a little prying, I discovered what I thought was a spirit attachment. When I looked closer, I realized something was terribly wrong.

Attached to her neck where I usually see spirit guides was a demon. I wasn't sure what to do at first; it had been the last thing I expected to find. I asked her all the standard questions, such as if she had been experiencing long-term illness or unexplained weakness, and she confirmed that indeed she had. My guide informed me it had been there for about seven years, and I asked her where she had been living at that time. She revealed she had been staying at a battered women's shelter a few states away. Suddenly it all clicked.

What we determined was that she had picked up a demonic attachment while there and it had been setting up shop inside of her energy body all that time. I discovered that it had started to affect another young female in the house recently with the same symptoms that seemed to inexplicably develop overnight.

Eager to take matters into their own hands, we worked together to come up with a plan. In this case, one where her son would help do most of the heavy lifting. The demon was misogynist and had no respect for women, so I had him perform a cleansing and exorcism on the house while she was in it. I had her and the other afflicted women take a series of cleansing baths over thirteen nights followed by another clearing on the house and counseling. I kept myself available in case they needed me, but they succeeded all on their own. I saw her a few months later, and she was a completely different person. A dark cloud had been lifted.

Usually by the time someone comes to me for help they are more in a cleanup phase and have missed the chance to take care of a problem before it became something they needed outside help with. In the case I just mentioned, we got lucky in finding the attachment before matters had gotten worse. I doubt she was expecting me to find it, but her guides and ancestors made it clear that something was wrong. My clients are proof that you can take matters into your own hands, and you can take your power back if you do the work. They are also a good example of how easily we can pick up unwanted vibes when we are experiencing stress, depression, and trauma.

In part 3, we are going to explore foundational and innovative techniques for cleansing bad vibes regardless of the situation you might be facing, and I am going to introduce you to the Scale of Cleansing. Combined with what we went over in the previous chapters, this section will provide everything you need in order to take on the bad vibes in your life.

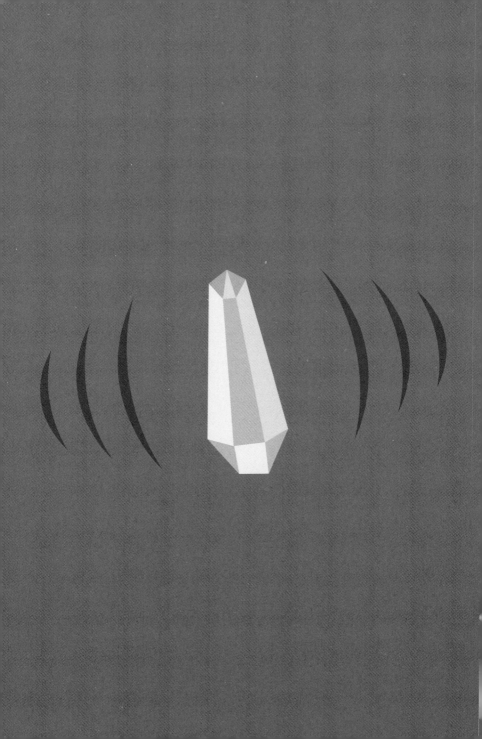

6

FOUNDATIONS OF
PSYCHIC CLEANSING

Among the metaphysical community, the concept of spiritual or psychic cleanliness has been a hot topic for quite some time. There are those who believe we should build up our spiritual immunity and that too much cleanliness can make us weak or ill-equipped to handle the struggles of life. Then there are those who make the simple argument that if we are going to take a shower to wash the filth of the day off each night, then why wouldn't we do something similar for our spiritual body? Spiritual cleanliness in those terms then becomes a matter of personal hygiene. I land somewhere in the middle of those two schools.

Spiritual and psychic cleanliness is something we should consider as part of our personal hygiene, and performing a spiritual cleansing is no less important than brushing our teeth. It is a way for us to keep our equipment in proper functioning order and how we keep larger problems from manifesting. While I agree that we need to develop thicker psychic skins, that is merely one part of gaining the upper hand as psychics. For those who are afflicted, it is a necessary step before relief can be found.

If you are new to the spiritual cleansing scene, this chapter grows on things we have already discussed and introduces you to meaningful practices that can make an impact immediately on your situation. If you have been around the block before, you will find a handful of topics and practices that might be new to you.

Let's dive in and discuss important cleansing practices that you should know as not only part of your personal hygiene routine but also as a means of introducing concepts that will be needed as we approach specific cases. Familiarize yourself with them, as they are not only providing the bedrock for a personal practice but also for how you will want to tackle the process with others, at locations, or on objects. These principles will grow to be useful in many ways, and I will elaborate on most of them later.

WORKING WITH SPIRIT ALLIES FOR CLEANSING

Our spirit allies are always with us and have a lot to teach us when it comes to the different ways we can work with our psychic abilities. I am always telling clients and mentees, if only as a reminder to myself, that our spirit allies are coaches and make excellent trainers. The more you spend time communicating and working with your ally, the stronger you will become. Admittedly, they really shine as protectors; however, they make fierce companions when battling bad vibes. We have already discussed how to meet them, let's look at the ways we can partner with them for spiritual cleansing.

In general, our main guides, the ones who work with us closely and over long periods of time, are going to help with identifying energies that are unwanted, especially if those energies are connecting to us. A good habit to develop is to check in with your allies a few times each week, just to ask if there are any connections that you should remove. Let them show you where to direct your energies. Similarly, when you go into any act of cleansing, it is a good idea to ask your guides to help you identify the vibes that need to go. They are tuned in to things we only can discover through them, so trust them.

On the other hand, there are allies that you can seek out or call to for help, specifically with the process of spiritual cleansing. Many religions have deities or spirits that are known for their power over negative energy, such as the Archangels Michael and Gabriel, for example. Because religions help to make up so much of our worldview, I always recommend looking to the religious background you are most comfortable with for ideas. If you aren't affiliated with any religion or are turned off by religion, you can always ask your guide to introduce you to another guide who can help you with this. It might sound silly, but like I said, they are better connected than we are.

I have a spirit ally who showed up one day when I was a young man. That was when I discovered that one of the things they do is eat bad vibes. They can swallow up minor spirits and spiritual energies, and that propensity has been a life saver. Yeah, it is weird, but it is cool, right? Mind you, I wouldn't work with a spirit who only lived off negative energy; they are likely to stir up trouble for you just so they can get a meal, but having an ally who is capable of such feats has been educational, to say the least.

CLEARING WITH SPIRITUAL ENERGY

We can clear spiritual and psychic energies by using those we might have access to. We have already done a bit of this work when I introduced you to the channeling and cord-cutting exercises, and we can build on those, modifying them to meet the needs of the moment. The more you practice those exercises, the stronger you will become and the easier it will be to remove unwanted vibes in the moment.

Our goal should always be to try and take care of bad vibes as they happen or at least shortly after, when we feel safe to do so. Developing a practice of clearing with energy allows you to respond pretty much anywhere without the need of some of the other things we will talk about in this chapter.

I am a major proponent of working with and developing a solid relationship with Source energy, as it is the great equalizer and has an unending potential for application. There are other forms of energy that have been discovered that can be worked with similarly and also offer their own modalities.

Working with systems such as Usui reiki or Blue Fire reiki lend themselves nicely to spiritual cleansing and have truly incredible things to teach us about moving energy and the interplay of the spiritual body and the physical world. I rolled my eyes every time someone brought it up for years because it sounded like a faith-healing scam, but I am now a convert. This isn't a book on reiki, and to practice any form of reiki you need to train with a teacher. Luckily for all of us, there are thousands of them out there; one is probably in your area, and far more qualified people than I have written extensively on the topic. Check out the recommended reading section in the back for my favorite books on reiki.

Aside from Source and reiki, there are many other forms of spiritual energy that can be called upon for cleansing. Most of the time, this requires us to become good friends with a bigger form of spiritual energy, such as a deity, an angel, or our ancestors. I always recommend working with your personal spiritual pantheon for this, especially in the beginning. For example, you can call upon the power of Christ and channel that energy if you have a connection with them. You can also call upon the power of a moon goddess, such as Isis, or the power of the women in your family through your matrilineal ancestry.

Being poly-spiritual, I like to make all the friends I can and call upon whomever is best for the job. I'm not a Christian, but Jesus and I are cool. I am not an Egyptian priest, either, but Isis and I go way back. I'm not saying to go out and appropriate a culture or work with a spiritual energy just because it has juice that you could gain access to. The most powerful bonds are those that are meaningful and resonate with your frequency.

CLEANSING WITH THE ELEMENTS

The unsung heroes of spiritual cleansing, especially outside of esoteric circles, are the elements. In the West, we know them as earth, air, fire, water, and spirit. Our system developed out of Greece thousands of years ago and has changed little since. In Chinese philosophy, the foundational elements are a bit different, sometimes referred to as agents, and are known as wood, fire, earth, metal, and water. This system coalesced sometime during the second century BCE and remains largely traditional to this day.

Like most Westerners, I was introduced to earth, air, fire, water, and spirit at a young age in cartoons and fantasy books. It wasn't until I got older and started to incorporate feng shui techniques into my life that I came across their Chinese counterparts. There is a lot of obvious overlap with the two, but they are actually very different in their approach.

What the Chinese system of agents offers that our Western system is often lacking is an understanding of how energy cycles from one stage of its existence to the next. In Chinese philosophy, this is known as *wuxing*, or five phases. Whereas our Western system is mostly concerned with form and substance, wuxing sees the elements as being concerned with process and quality. In the West, the elements are separate pieces of a whole, whereas in the East, they are phases of an unending cycle.

If we smoosh the two systems together, we can use the resulting information to tackle just about any problem, as both bring their own unique understanding of how the universe works. Please keep in mind that this is all my personal gnosis, and I am no Chinese philosopher.

What I present here is inspired by traditional teachings, not part of them.

EARTH

Grounding and stabilizing, the building blocks of matter and material existence. Earth energy is vital to all physical existence and manifestation on all realms. This energy is neutral and transitionary. Work with this energy as you physically clean a space to destabilize manifested bad vibrations. Earth energy also makes an excellent counter to chaotic energy or spirits that thrive on chaotic energy. It is also a good idea to bring earth energy into your clearing work if the case involves deception, lies, or betrayal, as it brings in the opposite vibrations of stability, honor, and fidelity. This energy is also ideal for combating or containing emotional energies.

WOOD

The first movement of matter into form, wood energy embodies the reflexive and generative properties of nature and matter. This energy is expansive and brings with it the vibrations of new life, spring, a renewal of vital forces, and sensuality. Work with wood energy to stimulate any body of psychic energy that has become stagnant or when there is residual emotional energy, making it excellent in haunting- and poltergeist-type situations. Think of wood energy not like a branch or a plank, but more so as growth and upward motion. In some schools, wood and air are interchangeable, but I see them as being distinctly different from one another, though they do overlap in vibration.

AIR

Air energy is comprised of space as well as the qualities of matter that are gaseous. Air exists beyond the physical yet is still part of the physical; it can be material but have no form. Thought and intellect, inspiration and communication, are all airy qualities that speak to the mind. Work with this energy in cleansings to help resolve bad vibes and attachments related to or causing depression, anxiety, cyclical thoughts, jealousy, fear, and nightmares. Air energy is ideal for combating the evil eye and similar vibes.

WATER

Water energy is emotional and conserving, deep and reflective, passive in small quantities but dangerous in large amounts; it has both supportive and destructive qualities. This energy is difficult to contain without earth energy (form) to support it and even that can be eroded with time. Water energy takes the form of whatever it is poured into. Work with this energy to find weak spots in spiritual armor and locations where energies are imbalanced. Include it in small amounts to erode attachments or sedentary energies or in large amounts to purify the spiritual body after it has been attacked. It is an ideal partner to combat vibes associated with rage or deviancies in sexual behavior as well as to destabilize energetic bonds.

METAL

Governing over vibrations that are rigid, persistent, determined, controlling, and forceful is the element of metal. This energy represents the tooling of matter, where thought (air) is given the ability to direct form (earth), as well as growth (wood). This can be positive or negative, depending on who benefits. While it is capable of great things, it can only do them with the help of the other elements. Metal energy epitomizes the peak of artistry while also heralding the beginning of the end to ingenuity and flexibility. I think of metal energy as being akin to the spiritual power of technology. Work with this energy when you experience resistance to your cleansing efforts, when violent acts have been committed at a location and the residual psychic imprint remains, and when you need to break through well-established vibratory patterns.

FIRE

Bold, intense, passionate, consuming, impulsive, as well as both creative and destructive, the element of fire is dangerous and unpredictable but can also be one of the most palpable when mastered. Fire energy is the ultimate catalyst for change and heralds both the beginning and the end of all cycles. It isn't an easy force to work with. By its nature, it doesn't like to be contained, which is why we usually only deal with it safely in small amounts. In spiritual cleansings, it is advised to work with this energy sparingly, and usually at the end, due to its unpredictability.

As a side note, it isn't a good idea to burn objects that you fear have an attachment or an unwelcome connection to the other side. While it might feel like an obvious end, it just frees up whatever energy was attached to the physical item, allowing it to move on to something else. If that item truly is haunted or has an attachment of some kind, you may just be helping that bad vibe proliferate by burning it. Instead, use the Scale of Cleansing to determine how to sever the attachment.

SPIRIT

Spirit is an animating force when it comes to its place as an element. It compels all of the other elements and can be found inside of them as well. I have already exposed you to this energy and described it earlier as "Source." It is this force inside of us that allows us to engage the spiritual aspects of the other elements. Spirit, as we know it traditionally, is a uniquely Western concept that views spirit as an actual substance.

EXERCISE FIFTEEN
Channeling the Elements

Now that we have reviewed the elements and have even expanded on them a bit, let's talk about working with them in spiritual cleansing. Connecting with these energies is a subtle experience that first is felt as an internal shift, such as feeling an emotion related to that element. As we tune in to that feeling and allow our awareness of it to expand, we allow for that energy to essentially spill forth onto our plane.

You might have noticed that with each description there were a lot of keywords that I used to help characterize them. This was so you had something simple to relate them to in your own life. Each of these elements corresponds to various experiences or people that embody the energies of those keywords to you. Review the descriptions one more time, this go around with the idea of relating them to aspects of your daily life. I always tell my students to "find the element inside you."

Once you have at least three corresponding aspects for each of the elements, take some time in meditation to review them internally. During this part of the exercise, do your best to identify an emotion that this element evokes when you review these three aspects. You don't need to worry about putting that emotion into words, but you do need to be able to identify it and recall it later. This is going to be completely different for each of us, depending on our past experiences. If I were to use the element of fire in a personal example, it would go something like this.

First Personal Aspect: Passion—unyielding focus on completing a task. I feel this when I write.

Second Personal Aspect: Destruction—uncontrollable rage that ends with emptiness. I felt this way when my father died.

Third Personal Aspect: Consuming—the drive to use
something up until it is gone. I feel this way about pizza.

So, what emotion do the aspects of my writing practice, my father's passing, and eating pizza all have in common? Longing. For me, the element of fire feels like longing, or more simply, wanting. I long to write a meaningful book that helps create real change in the world. I long for just one more hug from my father and to hear him laugh at one of my bad jokes. Silly yes, but I long to savor every single last atom of a good pizza; it would be my last meal if I had to pick one. I'm also lactose intolerant, so I haven't eaten a proper pizza in over a decade, forgive me this indulgence. I really long for cheesy deliciousness.

As you can see, these seemingly unrelated aspects of my life are connected to each other internally, or at least subconsciously. It doesn't have to make sense to other people, all that matters is that you understand the finer details for yourself when you do this part of the exercise. After you have reviewed each of the elements in this way, identifying emotions that correspond to them, we can move on to the easy part.

I call this last part easy because it isn't too different from the Source Star exercise. However, instead of reaching for Source energy, we are going to reach for one of the other elements. We do this by recalling the emotion we associated with that element and then allowing it to guide our thoughts until we psychically connect to it. We want to focus on this emotion so intensely that is washes over us, tinting reality for just a moment, so that we temporarily see everything through the lens of that emotion. As you do this, visualize that element springing forth from within you and taking form as a perfect sphere of pure energy above your head.

From here, you can channel and direct that energy as you would Source energy and it can be used as a replacement in the Lasers! exercise. Disconnect from the energy as you would Source energy.

There are even more elemental energies we can explore in this way; we aren't simply bound to using an old-school Western or Chinese model. We can work with any natural force if we are brave enough to venture and find it.

CRYSTAL AND MINERAL ALLIES FOR SPIRITUAL CLEANSING

The mineral kingdom is full of companions waiting to work with us, we only have to reach out and find them. Crystals can be worked with for spiritual cleansing purposes in a number of ways and there are several who come predisposed to help with such things. There are crystals that can help us channel energy and those that can help us by filtering or (for lack of a better term) sanitizing it. Both of which can make a massive difference in how we tackle or treat bad vibes.

Crystals such as black obsidian, clear quartz, ocean jasper, aquamarine, topaz, selenite, citrine, amazonite, sodalite, dumortierite, howlite, iolite, calcite, and labradorite are especially good at helping us to channel psychic energy efficiently while remaining grounded. I find it best to hold one of these while I perform cleansings or at the very least to have one of them on my person. Alternatively, you can place them around an environment to help energy move where it might be stuck.

Crystal companions such as Herkimer diamonds, citrine, shungite, amethyst, smoky quartz, selenite, petrified wood, fluorite, black tourmaline, onyx, and rhodonite make excellent filters. Place them in an area to help scrub environmental energy and carry them on your person to help keep unwanted energy from building up in the personal energy body.

Iron is perhaps the most famous of the mineral allies for its effectiveness against negative energy. Iron grounds out energy with lightning speed, making it useful not only for combating bad vibes but for times when there is an overabundance of vibrations and we are being hyperstimulated by them. I keep iron ore chunks around my home to disband unwanted energy and have a cuff that is made from iron that can be worn to assist in grounding.

Iron isn't necessarily something we have to go seeking out, we have iron in our blood, which can also be worked with for the same purposes. We call this process *iron activation*, and it is done to stimulate rapid grounding and energy clearing inside the body.

EXERCISE SIXTEEN
Iron Activation

The iron in our blood is what gives it the red color, and we are going to use that association to help in the activation process. To begin, ground as described in chapter 1 and stand with your legs shoulder width apart. Focus on your breath, those moments of stillness and silence that come in between inhale and exhale. Just breathe naturally and follow your breath, using it to lull you into a relaxed state.

Once you feel ready to move on, visualize a red ball of light emerging from your solar plexus. Next, take a series of three consecutive deep breaths, and with each exhale visualize that light growing brighter until it is so bright on the last breath that it fills the entire space you are in.

To complete the activation, breathe naturally for at least sixty seconds, visualizing this light dimming slowly as it is absorbed back into the body. This practice is especially useful when tackling things like curses or spirit attachments.

PLANTS, ESSENCES, AND OILS

The plant kingdom is part of our planet's natural spiritual metabolism and, provided we aren't allergic to them, they can be powerful aids for us as we expand spiritually. On a practical level, they help filter our air and produce oxygen while taking nutrients from the soil and using light to change those nutrients into sugar that it used to grow.

This cycle is something that we can tap into and work with by intentionally growing plants in areas where energy is stagnant. You can also bring several living plants into a location, and within the course of a few days, those plants will begin to metabolize the negative energy in that space. This alone is a great reason to have houseplants. Try growing philodendrons, ZZ plants, tradescantia, Scindapsus, Chinese evergreen, and snake plants for this purpose.

Plants can also lend us their vibration through their essences. An essence is the collected essential oils of a plant either suspended in water or alcohol (which is referred to as a *liquid essence*) or via direct extraction methods that render a pure product (an *essential oil*). This essence is believed to contain a distilled version of the spirit associated with the plant.

Traditionally, we release these essences when we burn them as a form of incense via an act of fumigation, wherein the smoke is used to release or stabilize energy. We can also do something similar by taking sacred baths. Both liquid essences and essential oils can be found at your local health food store, as well as tea alternatives for those interested in ingesting the plant's essence. It is not advised to ingest essential oils, and some liquid essences may be toxic, always do your research.

One of my favorite ways to work with plant essence is to suspend them in water and then put that mixture in a spray bottle that I can use to distribute it. Sometimes I make a tea and other times I just mix oils in with distilled water. Without an emulsifier, the oil and water will separate; however, if you shake the bottle well, they will incorporate.

A flower essence, which is a liquid essence taken specifically from the flowering part of the plant, is believed to contain the highest form of the plant's vibration, making this the part of the plant that is connected to Source. There are many varieties that can usually be internally taken, each capable of effecting our vibration in their own way. I recommend working with the flower essences of dandelion, St. John's wort, lavender, neroli, and sage for helping to remove unwanted spiritual vibrations attacking the spiritual body.

Whenever possible, I like to take a bath in a tea blended specifically for cleansing purposes. There are a handful of herbs that are particularly useful for cleansing purposes. Make a tea from them and use it in baths or as the water in your cleaning buckets when you clean your home. You can also powder them and sprinkle that powder where you need energy to disperse. Cooling herbs such as mint, spearmint, and eucalyptus are great for soothing and calming energy clearing, particularly for emotional psychic energy. Citrus plants such as lemongrass, lemon, and orange are great for breaking down unwanted energy.

CLEANSING BATHS AND SALT

Baths are a traditional form of cleansing and are included as a practical approach to resolving unwanted spiritual energy or for preparing the energy body to receive energy.

There are hundreds of recipes online and elsewhere, most containing the same basic components. Regardless of what goes into the bath, and I'll share several recipes over the course of this chapter, everything that goes into it must be intentional. It isn't merely enough to throw the ingredients in a bowl, we have to connect to psychic energy therein and assign it a purpose, ask it for help doing the heavy lifting. The philosophy behind how this works is simple, everything has vibration and is connected to a greater source. We can use our psychic skills to connect to that source through the items we are including in our bath.

To do this, I hold each ingredient, reach out with my consciousness to identify its vibration (for me this feels like grabbing something with my mind and holding it, for others it is done simply by breathing until that object feels as though it is part of them), and then giving it instruction by verballing telling it why I need its help and what I need it to do for me. It might feel silly, but by doing this we are acknowledging the indwelling spiritual being (some call them angels, plant spirits, or devas), which is often far more connected than we are. When all my ingredients are combined, I give them a group talk and explain the issue, then in the water they go.

When performing a cleansing bath, it is traditional to recite some sort of prayer to your god or spirit allies, asking them for guidance and help on the matter and also inviting them to become part of the process. If neither of those appeal to you, then recite one of the core belief sets from the first chapter.

EXERCISE SEVENTEEN
Simple Salt Cleansing Bath

You will need one cup of coarse sea salt. Rock salt or table salt also work. Epsom salt is not a suitable substitute, as it isn't really salt; in my experience, Himalayan salt does not work as well as plain white salt.

At low level of disturbance, salt should do the trick and there isn't a need for additional ingredients. Salt is a fantastic tool against bad vibes and, depending on how you apply it, a little bit can go a long way. Salt is one of the few natural substances that absorbs and disrupts etheric patterns. By taking a bath, we are using the natural conductivity of water to pull energy away from the body and salt to disrupt its connection. There is absolutely no science behind this, mind you; this is my best attempt at explaining how I think this tradition works. Regardless of what I think, salt baths just work!

Stay in as long as you feel you need to be there. Our intuition is a fantastic gauge for these things. I do recommend at least twenty minutes. When you are in the bath, perform the grounding exercise from the first chapter and other energy exercises, including those from this book. The idea is to activate your spiritual/energetic body as much as possible while you are bathing. When you're done, rinse the salt off.

Alternatively, if you don't have a bathtub, you can use the shower method. To do this, get a bowl of water big enough for your feet to go in, fill it up, and put the cup of salt in it. Remove anywhere from a cup to a third of the mixture and set aside. Soak your feet in the bowl, performing the energy exercises as described above. When you're finished, empty the contents of the bowl down any drain and hop in the shower, taking the reserved mixture with you. While under the running water, pour the mixture over your head (be sure to close your eyes), distribute it with your hands so that is coats your body, and rinse.

SONIC CLEANSING

Sonic/sound cleansing is a truly unique way to approach the process of spiritual clearing and, in my experience, is one of the most instantly effective techniques. I started using tuning forks and metal singing bowls to clear my crystal collection of energy after sessions and then quickly realized that the potentials were almost endless with the application. It turns out that a lot of other people had come to the same conclusion and that there is a huge market for sound cleansing tools. Now you can find everything from apps that let you do everything through a pair of headphones to reconstituted crystal singing bowls and chimes for when you want to feel the sounds move through you.

The principle of the technique is simple and, depending on how you look at it, as based in science as we can get for the subject. Sound is a physical phenomenon where vibration moves through some form of matter, be it liquid, solid, or gas, and most of us sense it audibly. If that vibration is strong enough, we can physically feel it travel through matter; kind of like when you stand too close to a speaker and can feel the air rumble or when you are playing an instrument and the note travels through its frame. Sound cleansing methods use that physical vibration to reset whatever it comes in contact with back to its natural state. For as long as the process endures, the sound will overpower any secondary vibration that is attached to an object or a location. Once the sound ceases, the object or location is no longer exposed to that vibration and will return to whatever its natural state is.

The nifty thing about this technique is that you can choose the instrument for the job that best suits you and your work. Tuning forks and singing bowls come in various tones and sound qualities. You can work with deep bass drums if you prefer rhythmic vibration or a didgeridoo to really feel the tone move through a space. You can even use a portable speaker and a keyboard app on your phone or use a midi player. Headphones work well when you are using sonic cleansing in meditation to help with mental and spiritual vibes. They aren't technically going to allow physical vibration to move through you, but they are useful when you have internal work to do.

There are many theories about what different tones can do and what specific audio frequencies are capable of. In my experience, the note played by the instrument doesn't necessarily matter as long as it is pleasing, and that is subjective. Higher tones (2000+ Hz) tend to be jarring for many of us, and their wavelengths are so fast that we can't necessarily feel them. Lower tones (>120 Hz) are usually more palpable in the physical sense, but they aren't as easy to hear for some folks. I recommend working somewhere in the middle (120–1900 Hz) range, which on a piano are octaves three through six, or an octave below middle C to three octaves higher.

EXERCISE EIGHTEEN
Sonic Clearing

The trick is that for this to work effectively, the sound should be a single tone that is sustained for thirty seconds to several minutes, depending on the situation. As a matter of everyday spiritual hygiene, thirty seconds will suffice. In cases where there is a major funk, we might be looking at a half hour and multiple sessions. In the field, this method needs to be applied to an appropriate degree matching the severity of the situation.

In homes or physical locations, it is best to target problem areas first and then work your way outward to the rest of the location before returning to the target areas to finish up. Spend two or three minutes in each room, moving the instrument of choice slowly around the room so that as much of the space can be exposed to the vibration as possible.

Smaller personal items need only around sixty seconds of exposure. A person, however, likely requires an hour to reset after an immediate attack and potentially multiple sessions if the problems are severe. If you are battling a long-term issue and have a lot of cleanup to do, multiple sessions that are done in accordance with other cleansing methods will likely be required.

GENERAL CLEANLINESS

Probably the most underrated element of spiritual cleanliness is the general physical state of the environment, object, or person. People who are psychically sensitive often tend to be the type to collect things, especially if there is a story or a sentiment attached. Everything has a vibration, of course, and sometimes we use the vibrations of the things we hold on to as a way of keeping ourselves protected from the outside world.

It is complicated, but there are clear correlations to mental and spiritual health and physical cleanliness, and we shouldn't take those lightly. We also know that negative energy and malevolent spirits like to hang out among clutter and chaos. If the environment is messy, cluttered, or items are being hoarded, all of that has to be resolved alongside any spiritual cleansing work. The two will help support the work of the other.

Scent also has a lot to do with how we perceive spiritual vibration. As humans, we have evolved to use our sense of smell to help us discern safety and are hardwired to avoid certain scents as a matter of self-preservation. Pet smells, along with those of blood, vegetable/wood rot, decaying animal tissue, mold, mildew, musk, char, feces, urine, and sweat are all commonly reported in cases of hauntings and spirit attachments. As a matter of general psychic cleanliness, it is a good idea to deep clean any areas where these smells may be present.

DEVELOPING A PERSONAL PSYCHIC CLEANSING ROUTINE

If you take what we have talked about up to this point, including everything from the first two parts, you have more than enough information to develop your spiritual/psychic cleansing routine, or at least to jazz it up if you already have one. That said, I realize I have thrown a lot at you and knowing just where to start might be a bit overwhelming, especially if you feel like you are under any form of spiritual attack.

Admittedly, my psychic cleansing routine is part of a bigger set of practices I regularly observe as part of my personal spiritual practice. This means that I think about it more than most people and have already found a way to prioritize it as part of my day-to-day lifestyle. That isn't likely going to be the case for everyone and, while I would love to tell you that you need to be going as hardcore as I tend to, the truth is that you probably don't.

By regular, I really just mean consistent and rhythmic. You don't need to take a cleansing bath every day, but you should ground and center your energy (as we discussed in part 1) daily. Save the cleansing baths for Friday or Saturday night when you can set some time aside and be truly present for the process. Several of my friends have syncopated their cleansing schedule to correlate with their hormonal cycle, other friends time their deeper workings by the moon. Developing a practice that fits into your rhythms is more important than trying to adjust those rhythms to the practice.

You should also feel free to use what works best for you and to skip what doesn't, especially after you have tried a method and realized it wasn't your thing. I still think you should try everything and stretch all of your psychic muscles, but ultimately doing a bunch of exercises that don't speak to you is only going to build resistance to the overall routine.

CONCLUSION AND JOURNALING

We went over a lot of information in this chapter and we have a lot more to go, however what we discussed here is an excellent starting point for understanding the nuances of spiritual cleansing work. As we build on these techniques, keep in mind that responding to bad vibes out in the world is a bit different than performing a regular cleansing routine. Each case will require a unique approach that is rooted in these foundational practices.

To help really make what we discussed here meaningful to you, respond to the following prompts in your journal.

1. Which elemental energy was the easiest for you to connect with? Which was the most difficult? Why do you think one (or more) of the elements was more difficult to connect with than the others?

2. What crystal and plant allies do you already have a relationship with? Do you think they would make good partners in your cleansing practice? Why or why not?

3. Based on your goals and familiarity with the exercises, create an outline for your spiritual cleansing routine. What do you think will be the most challenging aspect of the routine? How will you overcome that challenge?

7

THE SCALE OF CLEANSING, PART ONE

Do you ever find yourself dealing with unwanted frequencies and vibrations? Have you ever been overwhelmed by other people's psychic ick and thought, *There just has to be a better way!* Well, friend, I have news for you! The secrets of spiritual cleansing are yours for the low, low price of claiming your spiritual authority! That's right—you heard it here first, folks; this is a deal you surely won't want to miss out on! Act now while your sanity lasts!

Okay, all silliness aside, the scale is something else I came up with to help determine how best to move forward when cleansing and removing bad vibes that we discover during a scan. In truth, most of what we discussed in the previous chapter as foundational all constitutes what would be considered a level one cleansing when performed with an introductory skill level. We will address different ways to do this throughout this chapter and the next, but you've already done the groundwork, so to speak.

It's important to remember that any one of the bad vibes we discussed in part 2, as well as their causes, can present themselves in varying degrees at almost any point in our lives. In the next two chapters, we are going to take a closer look at the specifics of approaching, and ultimately clearing, those bad vibrations. This is the information that I wish I had when I was first starting out on my journey as a professional psychic medium and is a true distillation of two decades of experience. My methods might seem odd to some, but you will find methods here that provide meaningful results regardless of your skill level. The scale is designed to help you tackle the problem regardless of severity, provided you remember these four core concepts about using it.

THE SCALE IS CUMULATIVE

As the scale progresses from level one to level five, the requirements for cleansing the vibration and/or its cause will increase. Each level on the scale represents additional work that needs to be performed to get the job done. This means that to remedy a level three situation, the work for levels one, two, and three must be done.

At a minimum, it is recommended that something is done for each of the three parts of being: the mind, the body, and the spirit. Regardless of the level at which you choose to respond, all three of those elements must be cleansed in order for the cleansing to be effective overall. It might feel laborious to approach a cleansing from three separate directions, but this thoroughness ensures results.

THE SCALE OFFERS MULTIPLE APPROACHES

I've done my best to include as many methods as I can fit into this chapter and the next, but ultimately which ones you choose and how you apply them is up to you. Not every technique is going to fit every unique situation. Feel free to follow the instructions to the letter or to draw inspiration when you see fit. Outlined will be recommendations for how to respond mentally, physically, and spiritually at each level.

IT IS PART OF A SYSTEM

The scale is designed to help us clear bad vibes, but to keep them away, protection and transmutation techniques must also be applied. After you've applied those techniques, you will also likely find that repetition of these cleansing techniques is required. Healing and fortification of the spiritual body takes time. We will go over protection and transmutation in part 4.

IT ADDRESSES VIBRATION AND FREQUENCY AS PSYCHIC PHENOMENA

Everything boils down to energy, and these techniques approach bad vibes, even the preternatural ones, as energy that can be disconnected from. Sometimes we will be able to yank the plug out (so to speak) on our own, and other times we will need help from spiritual allies or physical ones. The key to remember is that these problems are universal and affect us regardless of religion or spiritual philosophy.

Feel free to add elements of your religious foundation, especially if you feel spiritually empowered by it. Invite Buddha, Jesus, your ancestors, angels, and anyone else along that you think should be there for you. I will endeavor to provide these methods without religious context and when I do butt up against it, I will provide alternatives that have worked for me in the past.

I have done my fair share of spiritual cleansings and, regardless of what school of thought you follow or your spiritual background, everything boils down to energy and how we interact with it at the end of the day. This can be maddening at times, making things feel more complicated, but in reality, it means that the rules of engagement are pretty straightforward when it comes to spiritual cleansing. To remove, overwrite, wash away, or dissolve energy of any kind, we must use a stronger energy source.

This is why taking your authority and working on yourself are so important. The clearer you are about who you are and what you want, the stronger your vibration will be when coming up against other vibrations that might mean you harm.

The scale is designed to help you know what to do when you approach different levels of difficulty. It comes from decades of experience and is meant to give you a blueprint for how to deal with issues that arrive while remaining in a position of power. My methods are a little different from others in that I endeavor to remedy the cause behind the symptom, which requires a unique approach at times.

I believe in the power of the mind, in the power of conditioning the mind, and in the power of a strong resolve. Recite the core beliefs over and over until you have convinced yourself that you have all the power, and the bad vibes are about to find out what happens when they mess around. You have to know that you are in control.

Before we jump in, I want to remind you that I mentioned severity level when discussing the individual types of bad vibes we might encounter during the last part. Use that information as it relates to the different levels on this scale when developing your plan of action.

LEVEL ONE: MILD DISTURBANCES

Bad vibes that produce minimal ambient stress, anxiety, and tension fall in level one. These vibrations are subtle unless you bring attention to them and can possibly be connected to larger issues within the spiritual ecosystems we move through. These bad vibes are usually unintentional and environmental, and our energetic reflex to them goes unnoticed as part of our regular ups and downs. They become a problem when they accumulate over a period for any reason.

Usually, level one disturbances manifest from a lack of energetic movement internally or within the location/environment. Possible sources include the self, empathic sludge, etheric cords, rude energy, and residual energy. These are the vibes we pick up easily and should be handled as part of our regular spiritual hygiene.

We reflexively respond with mood shifts, increased emotional sensitivity, repetitive or unending thoughts, and physical stress. These vibes cause us to feel like we are having a bad week, are unlucky, and incapable of achieving goals, as well as needlessly confused.

If these symptoms last longer than a week, you should consider a level two cleansing.

HOW TO PHYSICALLY RESPOND

Much of how we would go about tackling this level from a physical perspective involves stimulating the natural flow of energy in the body or location. This increased energetic circulation will help flush out internal stagnant energy or energy that might have been passing through and got stuck.

In a person, we do this by getting the body moving and, whenever possible, engaging in new surroundings. The goal here is to break routine and to stimulate our senses. If able, go for a walk, spend some time outdoors, and take your shoes and socks off and let your feet touch the earth directly. Find ways of increasing your heart rate naturally in short increments, and drink lots of water.

In locations, we do this by opening windows, turning fans on, and bringing light to dark spaces, even if temporarily. Burning copal or dragon's blood resin over charcoal helps to flush out energies through fumigation. Safely burn a little in each space until the area smells like the incense in each corner, or by slowly moving the incense around the space from room to room.

HOW TO MENTALLY RESPOND

The mind is a powerful thing, and it may be responsible for this vibe, or at least contributing to it. Level one bad vibes tend to trap us into cycles of repetitive thinking and unending thoughts. By this I mean overthinking things, thinking about the same thing repeatedly, or thinking about something but never coming to a conclusion about it. These cycles of thought give the source of the bad vibe energy to continue and construct a negative view of reality, which ultimately furthers that vibe's sphere of influence.

Respond by choosing creative and critical thinking over the cycles and seek closure. This might take a few attempts, but the idea here is to break the connection and give your brain a chance to form new connections. Creative thinking, the kind that's used to make art and to solve puzzles, helps us to reformat strategy and reframe problems. Essentially, it helps us to flip the script and find new pathways ahead. Paint a portrait, do some crochet, write a poem, solve some Sudoku. Activating different parts of our brain is not only grounding but also invigorating.

EXERCISE NINETEEN
Reorientation

Reorientation is a critical thinking exercise I use to help make sure all of my mental energy is lined up and headed in the right direction. Critical thinking helps us put the problem into digestible, subjective terms, which gives us the tools to find a conclusion. This allows us to complete our thought process and to reorient the energy we are otherwise spending on it. Think of your mental energy like a river and the cycles of thought like a dam that is blocking that energy. This exercise helps to open the floodgates. The key is to face whatever it is that is difficult about the situation we are mentally chewing on and to set a boundary for how long we are going to continue to chew on it and in what way.

I do this by setting dedicated time aside to meditate on the matter and make sure to set two timers when I do. For the first ten to fifteen minutes, I try to think about it from as many perspectives as possible, as subjectively as possible. You might need longer to get all the way through the process, which is fine, but set a time limit and stick to it.

I ask myself a few questions like:

1. What would this person I am upset with say about the situation if they were being honest with themselves? Is the situation because of someone else at all?

2. How have I helped or harmed myself or my cause by spending mental energy on the matter as I have been?

3. Do I feel shame or guilt related to this matter? If so, why?

4. What parts of the situation am I honestly responsible for, if any? How do I take responsibility for those things?

5. What parts of the situation are honestly out of my control? How does that make me feel?

6. What is the best possible outcome for the situation? What will it take to make that happen? What parts of that are in my control?

7. What is the worst outcome for the situation? What will it take to change that?

8. What am I going to do if I never receive closure on the matter?

I set another ten- to fifteen-minute timer and then go about the business of making decisions regarding how I feel and what I am going to do about the matter. By this point, the answers usually present themselves quickly, as all of the work preceding this has helped to frame the situation into smaller pieces. To reach these conclusions, I ask myself the following questions:

1. Why am I invested in the outcome of this situation? What does this say about me?

2. How am I vulnerable in this situation?

3. What are three concrete facts, not opinions, about this situation that work in my favor?

4. What are three concrete facts, not opinions, about this situation that work against my favor?

5. What is the deep lesson for me to learn? (Try not to make this shallow. Like, don't do the "to not trust people" thing. It's bypassing and boring. Think harder. Think meaningful. Perhaps instead of the lesson being not to trust others, it's that you are vulnerable to the influences of others and you need to establish better boundaries.)

6. What are at least three actionable steps that I am going to take in order to achieve the best possible outcome?

7. What are at least three actionable steps I am going to take in the worst-case scenario?

After this, I am done and usually feel a great sense of relief—it's like stretching after being cramped up for too long in a car headed nowhere. The point of this exercise was to figure out the puzzle to the best of your ability and to come up with actionable items that will best help you as you move forward. After this, there shouldn't need to be much further thought unless it is to adjust your plan, but in general this should ease stress and provide a plan of action, breaking negative thought patterns.

HOW TO SPIRITUALLY RESPOND

Spiritually speaking, we want to support the work we are doing mentally and physically by performing clearing work to help remove energy that is being brought up and released. An excellent way to do this is to take an intentional cleansing bath and to perform cord cuttings on ties that no longer serve us.

It is important to pay special attention to personal energy levels and to adjust behavior if needed in order to make a clean break from the level one bad vibe. Look over the foundational exercises from the previous chapter for inspiration.

LEVEL TWO: THE DARK CLOUD

These are bad vibes that are channeled through a person or an object via etheric connections. The person affected might not be aware of it. They may just feel like a dark cloud is hanging over them or sense that their presence is unwelcome by others, causing them to withdraw. In these cases, the bad vibe that we are tuned in to is altering our frequency and making us feel out of sync with those that we normally are in sync with. If sufficient dark cloud psychic energy is present near a physical object, it can be absorbed and later released, making the item a transmitter of its source. Any jewelry regularly worn should be cleansed.

The big differences between level one and two are that level one situations are isolated and ambient. They aren't focused or being brought through a person's psychic field directly. With level two, the bad vibes are focused and are being directed through some sort of psychic agent. This happens as a result of internal struggle or after a level one bad vibe has had time to fester and set up shop within a person's energy field.

As you might guess, level two cleansings address the initial connections that lead to things such as spirit attachment. Level two cleansings are recommended to anyone who regularly works with spiritual medicine, who interacts with the spirit/psychic world intentionally (especially if they are not familiar with it), and who has visited locations where bad vibes congregate.

Use your intuition on that. If you've been to a place where people were murdered or a war broke out, known haunted locations, your cousin Eddy's basement where he cooks meth, anywhere that makes you feel spiritually unsettled, that's where bad vibes congregate.

These disturbances are usually linked to a psychic person who is not in spiritual balance, likely they tapped into a spiritual source accidentally and hasn't separated from it effectively. This is very common for those with expressed empathic abilities. This is also common for those who are untrained psychic sensitives as well as those who dabble disrespectfully in the occult.

To effectively respond, the agent should undergo a level one cleansing in addition to what is suggested here. Again, use your discretion, but do try to cleanse the vibration on a physical, mental, and spiritual level.

HOW TO PHYSICALLY RESPOND

To be as effective as possible, the agent should undergo the same processes as level one, but repetitively. This means they should develop an exercise routine instead of relying on one intense round. This will not only support the more deliberate work you'll be doing mentally and spiritually but also will help to speed the process along. My general rule of thumb is twenty-one days. This is long enough for new habits to be learned and old ones replaced.

Objects should be cleaned to remove dirt and debris if possible and then brought under running water for five minutes or longer. Five minutes is long enough for some effect to take place, but the longer the better. If possible, a natural stream will be the most effective, but what comes out of the tap will do! When you're finished, fumigate the item as described in level one by passing it through the smoke.

HOW TO MENTALLY RESPOND

If you do a Source scan and find that you are the agent these vibes are coming through, then you should perform the Source Scan exercise, if possible. The chances are high that there are clues as to what the original source of these vibrations actually is, which gives you a direct path to resolving the matter. If the person is someone else, try to talk to them if you can about what is on their mind, otherwise hand them this book and dog-ear the Source Scan page for them. (It's okay, I said so. But only for this book.)

If it is a physical item, then wrap it in black fabric. This will subtly dampen its influence, as black absorbs color and has traditionally been used to effectively absorb negative energy for quite some time. It also has the effect of removing the item from sight and, as the saying goes, out of sight, out of mind.

HOW TO SPIRITUALLY RESPOND

Level two bad vibes are particularly rooted in the psychic. Regardless of whether you are the agent these vibes are coming through or someone else is, the person responsible needs to get a better grip on their psychic abilities. This type of disturbance is a clear sign of rogue psychic energy and that can be avoided with proper training. Check out the recommended reading section on psychic development in the back for my favorite psychic development books.

If left unchecked, this same set of circumstances can be a breeding ground for poltergeist and moderate spirit attachments. There is already a good chance that low-level spiritual wildlife is noticing the excess of energy. If allowed to continue, it can also attract stronger spiritual entities that may be difficult to remove.

Essentially, our goal with a level two cleansing is to remove connections that have been made without our consent and to clear unwanted energy traveling via our existing etheric connections. A level two cleansing is ideal for use if you are someone who interacts with psychic energy in a direct manner on a regular basis, as it also helps to resolve psychic debris. Here are two energy exercises I use when performing this level of cleansing.

EXERCISE TWENTY
Source Star for Self and Immediate Surroundings

Perform the Focusing and Connecting to Source exercise from chapter 1. At the end, visualize Source energy collecting as a dense ball of liquid light at the center of your solar plexus. Notice that as it forms, it illuminates all connections that are made to you. They look like silver strands stretching out in all directions. Some of these are clear to you, these are welcome connections that have purpose for you. Other connections remain aloof no matter how much you focus on them; they are so fine that you might not even acknowledge them without them being illuminated by Source light. That ball of Source light isn't just a tiny lamp, it is a star brimming with potential.

When ready, breathe slow and deep and allow this ball to grow larger with each exhale until it expands to encompass your entire physical being. Then, push this liquid ball outward so that it fills your immediate surroundings, until eventually it fills the space where you are. Notice that as the light expands and touches the world around you it disintegrates those connections that remained fuzzy and unclear to you. Let the light swirl around you as a torrent of Source energy and allow it to cleanse these connections from your energy body.

Notice that the light touches your welcomed existing connections to others with gentleness and invigorates them to be stronger in return. It brings clarity to them and eliminates all negative energy sent between you and those people that has made its way into your reality.

When you are finished, take three deep breaths, allowing the liquid light to slowly fade as it is absorbed by your spiritual body. Once complete, it is a good idea to perform a simple grounding.

A SPECIAL NOTE ABOUT CURSES

The average curse, intentional or otherwise, usually rests here at a level two disturbance. The power in curses comes with the belief in them, and curses know how to make themselves look a lot bigger and scarier than they actually are. Out of all forms of bad vibes I have encountered, I would say that curses are the smartest and most cunning. They spring out of an intelligent life-form, and I think because of that they possess a degree of intelligence themselves, or perhaps they remain connected to their place of origin and use the available intelligence there. Either way, curses make us think we are in danger and prey upon our spiritual nature.

The degree of disturbance caused by a curse is directly proportional to the amount of energy it is able to amass. That means you have to disconnect from it and keep your mind away from the energy it is producing. I cannot stress that enough. In addition to a nice salt bath, perform the Iron Activation exercise from the previous chapter, and spend time connecting to things that inspire you and do your best to avoid giving in to repetitive thoughts or ennui. If the disturbance is larger and its effects are widespread, treat it as though it were a spirit attachment and not a curse.

EXERCISE TWENTY-ONE
Curse Removal

The surefire way to remove a curse from someone afflicted by them is to take a series of three baths, each meant to purify a different layer of your spiritual anatomy. Before the baths, perform the Iron Activation exercise and recite your core beliefs. During each of these baths, perform the Source Star exercise.

The first bath should use a healthy amount of salt—I usually go for a pound for a full bathtub. The second should have about a liter of milk added to a full bath, goat milk is traditional, and you should soak for at least fifteen minutes. The last bath needs to be more of a shower, in that you need to stand under running water when performing the exercise. When all three are done, any curses that were placed on you should be detached from your vital energies. Perform a level one cleansing on your space afterward.

LEVEL THREE: THE DARK TOWER

Level three disturbances are similar to level two but on an environmental level. These are disturbances that are linked to specific locations and can be the result of human involvement or naturally occurring phenomena, such as ley lines. These are locations where energy has pooled and has festered, adversely affecting those who come in contact with it. These locations are not haunted—we aren't quite there yet—but they do feel heavy and often leave those who travel through them physically weakened.

Level one disturbances are often tied to level three disturbances, the former being the result of interaction with environments with dissonant energy. Dark towers (locations that emit bad vibes) are much more common than we might think. Offices, malls, schools, homeless shelters, and elderly care facilities are notorious for becoming dark towers as a result of the type of energy that traffics through them. However, dark towers can also be abandoned buildings or places where energy hasn't moved properly for an extended period of time.

Dark towers are havens for lower-level spirit forms that are passing by and make for good examples of places where the worlds merge as a result of the spiritual gravity collected within them. These places can become haunted by rogue spirits, but typically they do not house spirits for too long and generally do not have spirits that originate from their locations. Residual hauntings, where psychic energy has been recorded onto a location, are considered a form of level three disturbance and can be corrected through a specialized cleansing process known as *positive imprinting*.

Although dark towers are not producers of preternatural phenomena, they do attract preternatural attention. As a precaution, when you encounter a level three disturbance it is important that you reinforce your personal protections and that you perform a level one cleansing or equivalent once you leave.

To effectively clear the space, multiple level three clearings might be required. It is vital that you check back on the space a week after the cleansing, perform a refresh of the cleansing work where needed. Then check in once more a month later to do the same. If the disturbance is well established, the location will remain vulnerable without follow-up care. We have to essentially treat the space like a wound, drain off the infection, and then tend to it for a few months after to ensure it heals properly. Usually, however, one thorough level three cleansing will take care of most of the problem, if not entirely. Still, we must check in after to ensure our work is done.

HOW TO PHYSICALLY RESPOND

It is generally a good idea to physically clean the space, scrubbing floors and walls to remove grime and reduce any accumulated filth. Cleaners containing the essential oils of lemon, pine, or orange are especially great for helping to break through residual psychic energies. Be sure to open windows to get energy moving and to "air out" the space.

To help drain off the collected bad vibes, place iron in the center of the space and around its perimeter. You'll need at least three pieces for the perimeter, but you can use as many as you feel the need to beyond that. The goal is to create a geometric shape that can encircle the space. Leave the iron in place while you perform the cleansing, and it will ensure the energy is properly grounded. Retrieve it when you are finished; do not leave it in the space unless you have detected a specific location where energy struggles to ground (closets, utility rooms, and windowless spaces are notorious for being energy traps).

Make the space as bright as possible, filling it with as much light as you can. Burn cleansing herbs and incense like we discussed in the previous chapter.

Place bowls of salt around to help break up energy. You can add cleansing essential oils and dry herbs to make them more efficient and help you hide them in plain sight; most people assume its potpourri.

Additionally, placing crystal and mineral allies near the entrances and exits to move energy along, like those we discussed in the previous chapter, would be especially helpful during the recovery process.

EXERCISE TWENTY-TWO
Positive Imprinting

This is an exercise that should only be done once a thorough level one cleansing has been done on a space. In extreme cases, you might need to perform this work three or four times over a year if problems persist.

When battling energy that is deeply rooted in a location, you can essentially write over the existing psychic energy and replace it with a new one. This is something I started experimenting with years ago, and it really changed the game. This is now the only way I approach residual energies and residual hauntings. Before you begin, perform a level one cleansing on the space.

The concept is simple: gather a bunch of friends and have a party. Get everyone happy and joyful, laughing and full of positive energy. Then, when everyone is at their peak, have the group go around the home and touch the walls. As they do this, they will be imprinting that energy onto the home.

When tackling residual hauntings, perform this working as close to the time of the regular phenomena as possible. Again, this might require a few applications throughout the year, but once it has a chance to take effect, it can really flip the script on a bad situation.

HOW TO MENTALLY RESPOND

At this level, the space suffers from a disturbance that generates and feeds off moods, fear, anxiety, depression, and just about all the bad thoughts you can think of. To combat this, the space needs to undergo a bit of a makeover to create interference for those patterns. To do this, I recommend people start by playing uplifting music and finding a way to fill the space with laughter.

If it is a space that is frequently occupied by a regular group of people, such as an office, then stimulate conversation among those there regarding the bad vibes they feel. Ask them if they feel anything off about the building, if they have had any preternatural experiences there. Getting people talking to one another about the psychic ecosystem can be an incredible help for shifting the overall paradigm.

HOW TO SPIRITUALLY RESPOND

The pooling energy must be drained (grounded) and the space it was occupying cleared. My two favorite ways of making this happen allow for you to do this work expeditiously or at a slower pace, which might better suit some situations. Let's discuss.

The risk of resurgence with a level three disturbance is quite high, as is the risk for level four and five disturbances. The reason being that the cause of the disturbance must be repeatedly addressed until new pathways for the energy to drain can develop. This is why I stress the importance of aftercare and responding with a multipronged approach. To successfully resolve a level three disturbance, you must find the cause and remove it, when that is not possible, then we have to rely on slower, targeted applications of clearing in order to resolve the issue effectively.

Right now, the level three disturbance is a lot like a psychic abscess, and it needs to be drained. Gross, right? We can go in and burst the bubble aggressively, draining off as much as possible in one visit, or we can slowly drain it off over the course of weeks or months. The best approach for homes, offices, and places where there tends to be a lot of traffic is to do as much at one time and then to rely on therapeutic measures and aftercare to finish the job. For natural spaces or spaces where the energy collected is older, or possibly better established (think odd patches of land, abandoned homes, and so forth) then often the best approach to stimulate the environment is to do the heavy lifting over time, which will allow for a healthier ecosystem in the end.

I am going to present to you three methods for draining energy out of a space. Each require you to respond mentally and physically, as instructed previously in order for them to be successful. The first two methods work as standalone procedures and can be tailored to your specific disturbance. The last method is a mix of both methods and, while it might be a little overkill in some situations, will make sure the job gets done and that the natural balance in the space is restored.

EXERCISE TWENTY-THREE
Iron Plug (Slow Method)

This exercise uses an iron nail or a piece of iron ore to ground energy directly into the earth. To successfully do this, it needs to be buried at least 50 percent into the soil. Iron is a natural grounding agent that will pierce the psychic bubble in a specific location and allow for it to drain off. Ideally, this would be in the center of the disturbance; however, this is rarely possible. The alternative is to put iron in the ground near the entrances of the location and then have a piece simply sitting (not buried) in the center of the disturbance. The iron will pull at the accumulated energy and eventually break it up over time, draining it off into the iron placed at the entrances.

Placing iron at the entrances is also an effective way to keep energy from accumulating, in general. I often recommend it as a protective measure.

If you are treating an apartment or a cubical, placing unburied iron at the entrances of your unit, as well as in the east and west, will help to disrupt psychic energy. That energy must be cleared manually with level one cleansings regularly (daily or every other day) during treatment or it will simply move to another unit and likely come back.

The iron plug is a great trick that doesn't require much spiritual thinking to get the job done. The iron, by virtue of its own properties, will do most of the hard work for us. The only caveat is that the land around the disturbance must be healthy enough to process the energy being channeled into it. A sign that it is in good health is that there are living plants and trees and natural fauna in the area. If there is no living flora or fauna in the area, you are likely dealing with the level four or five disturbance.

EXERCISE TWENTY-FOUR

Creating a Ley Line Tributary (Faster Method)

We will discuss ley lines in depth in the next chapter, as they are an entire field of study on their own that is worth a closer examination. For now, think of ley lines as channels of psychic energy that travel through the planet like veins and arteries. They collect and distribute energy, ultimately filtering it and reusing it as part of the greater spiritual ecosystem of the planet. We can create temporary tributaries to them that can effectively drain off the accumulated energy into a natural vein of similar energy somewhere in the earth.

This is different from working with iron in that it will require some of that projective psychic work on your part. It also does not rely on the surrounding environment to absorb and process the energy.

To do this, you first need to find a ley line. There is a chance that you already know where one is. If you are curious, you can probably google your location with ley line in the search find and a map of close ley lines other people have found and are working with. For hardcore ley line enthusiasts, there is a belief that some ley lines deal with specifically positive energy and others specifically negative. This is said to account for why some areas in the world vibrate with a particularly high or low frequency.

My way around this is to rely on rivers and their tributaries as a method for ensuring that the energy gets picked up as it naturally would. Ley lines follow all major rivers, and the moving body of water will force the energy to break apart. This method is the safest way to ensure that the energy is not allowed to move elsewhere and become stagnant.

Before you begin, look at a map of your area and find the nearest river, large stream, or ocean. Look for existing tributaries that might be close to your location, it is okay if there aren't any.

Find the disturbance in your location and stand as near as possible to its center, facing the direction of the nearest tributary or large body of moving water. Perform a personal grounding and part one of the Lasers! exercise from the first chapter. Instead of allowing the Source energy to flow through your hands, however, direct it through the core of your body and out through your perineum. If that sensation is difficult or uncomfortable, move the energy out through the arches of your feet. It is important to see this energy move as a solid stream from above you.

Next, direct the energy to tunnel down into the earth deep enough that you sense bedrock, and then visualize a laser beam of Source energy traveling from that location directly to the moving water. Once I feel connected to the water, I open my channel to Source as wide as possible and flood the disturbance with fresh Source energy. Remain in that position, channeling the energy off to the water and its ley line, until you no longer sense the disturbance. When you are done, scan your energy body and direct any bad vibes that you might sense have stuck to you in the process, if any, and release them to the channel.

To finish, pull your energy upward from the bedrock and, when you feel your energy return to a state of present-mindedness, open your eyes and disconnect from Source. You will want to perform a level one cleansing bath on yourself after. Be aware that this process can be draining to perform and might exhaust you the first few attempts. Over time, your projective abilities will strengthen, and this won't have the same affect.

EXERCISE TWENTY-FIVE
Etheric Stent

This exercise is a hybrid of the last two and is a fantastic way to handle long-term disturbances and help the natural spiritual ecosystem reestablish itself.

Perform the last exercise with a piece of iron in front of you. Instead of pulling your energy back up to yourself at the end, direct it into the piece of iron. This will have the immediate effect of interfering with your channel, which is exactly what you want. For now, the energy lines you created are still active, they are just sort of tied off there at the iron. At this point, you no longer need to feed energy into the working; instead, visualize the energy draining off through iron and directly to the nearest tributary via that laser beam in the bedrock.

Leave the iron there at the center of the disturbance, add extra pieces near an entrance and bury them in the ground halfway. Come back in a few days to check on the progress. It is likely that for smaller disturbances the stent will need to remain in place for around twenty-eight days, or a lunar cycle. For larger disturbances, it might take several months or the changing of a season, possibly even a year. To quicken the process, be sure to perform regular level one type cleansings on the space.

A SPECIAL NOTE ABOUT VORTICES

Technically, vortices are a level three disturbance, but they fall just outside of the realm of the normal. I provide a more flushed-out examination in the following chapter; however, it is worth putting a note about them here. In short, vortices are caused when the perfect conditions are met and different types of moving energy collide. As cheesy as it sounds, the tornado is a great analogy for how a vortex works. Different streams of air with different temperatures meet when the right circumstances are provided and a very natural phenomena occurs.

Vortices aren't just thin places in the walls between worlds caused by the right type of energy collecting in the right way, they are open doorways between the worlds. They come in varying degrees of intensity, and some are more capable of piercing through the worlds than others. Vortices are rarely stable, though they do tend to appear in the same place when those conditions are met.

For the most part, vortices appear naturally, but they are incredibly rare. The general advice is to leave them alone; however, in the event that you ever need to temporarily turn one off, there is something you can do. The safest way to turn off a vortex is to disrupt the conditions that make it possible to manifest in the first place. You can put iron in a sporadic pattern (avoid a circle shape or a geometric pattern) in the area of the vortex, but do not attempt to flush the energy of the vortex. Simply allow the iron to break up the conditions of the environment. This is likely only a temporary measure. The more iron, the better. Salt is too temporary to be of any use. There is no exact science for this, but depending on the strength of the vortex, this application should last at least a few days. There are more aggressive ways to close off vortices; however, they require their own book.

CONCLUSION AND JOURNALING

In this chapter, I introduced you to the Scale of Cleansing and further clarified some of the finer details related to successful spiritual cleansing. If you were to take only one thing from this chapter it should be that we must approach this process from three levels: the mind, the body, and the spirit.

Ultimately, the bad vibes we face directly in the wild are different from those we might face as a matter of our regular spiritual hygiene, but our responses will always be rooted in the same drive to bring the related situation back to a place of harmony. In the next chapter, we are going to continue to develop the scale as we learn to approach some of the stranger elements of the spiritual and the psychic.

Break out your journal and write about any of the topics we discussed in this chapter that stuck out to you and about any bad vibe experiences you have had that might be related to them. Knowing what you know after reading this chapter, how might you go about treating those bad vibes?

8

THE SCALE OF CLEANSING, PART TWO

In this chapter, we are going to discuss best practices for cleansing vibrations related to hauntings, poltergeists, and attachments. We will explore different severity levels for these occurrences as well as what makes one method of clearing more effective than another. Keep in mind that the scale is cumulative. When using it, your response should include a form of cleansing from the levels that came before it to ensure relief from affliction.

LEVEL FOUR: HAUNTINGS AND POLTERGEISTS

I refer to this level as the breaking point because we start moving into what I consider to be preternatural territory. Here the lines blur between what are normal energetic variables, such as energy getting stuck or needing to rid ourselves of personal blocks and connections that are weighing us down, to the realm of the uncanny and preternatural.

In a level four disturbance, the location has amassed enough psychic energy to either produce or house conscious forms of psychic energy such as spirits, ghosts, apparitions, and poltergeist. Level four disturbances can be fixated on a person, a place, or a thing; however, they aren't necessarily a bad thing. What is good or bad in these instances is up to you and your comfort levels. The main difference between a level three and a level four disturbance is intelligence.

Conscious psychic energy is a psychic body of energy that has some degree of mind to them. Most have limited to no understanding of themselves outside of their impulses, much like a lower animal species. These energies can look like they possess intelligence, but upon closer inspection there is none to find. They react instinctively and out of an impulsive will to survive.

Sentient psychic energies are conscious psychic energies that are self-aware (to some degree) and can communicate their needs. Both types of phenomena can be found at a level four disturbance.

If the conscious psychic disturbance is satiated at its location, meaning it can harvest enough energy to carry on, it will likely choose to remain in that location. If, however, it is unable to sustain itself, it can move on its own accord to another location or attach itself to a person or an object.

Let's take a look at how level four disturbances can manifest and what to do about them.

IN PEOPLE...

Level four disturbances that are connected to people can originate from that person or from outside of them. The most common form of level four disturbance in people is what is referred to as a "spirit attachment," wherein a spirit develops a parasitic relationship with a host and feeds off of their vital energies. These can quickly turn into farming situations where the parasite jumps from person to person in a home or a friend group.

Most spirit attachments are thoughtforms, hungry ghosts, and/or elemental beings. In the rarest of instances, the spirit can be demonic in nature, in which case you are dealing with a level five disturbance.

Spirits, such as ghosts, can also come to haunt people they were close with. When we are comfortable with their presence, we consider it a blessing, but when we aren't we deem ourselves haunted.

Spirit attachments are easily picked up when we are weak in body, mind, or spirit, using our soft spots as access points to our vital energies. This makes us particularly susceptible to attack when we are already vulnerable.

Level four disturbances can also manifest as a result of hyper psychic activity and may not be related to a spirit at all (*see* Poltergeist).

IN PLACES AND OBJECTS...

In locations, level four disturbances are particularly interesting in that the amount of energy that had to amass to make them possible is actually quite astounding. The difficulty is in communicating with them to figure out what type of spirit they are.

When sentient psychic energy, such as a spirit, emerges from the location, we consider it a haunting. In this, the spirit is attached to the location as a result of massive psychic imprinting. In the case of ghosts, the person had to have had a major connection to that location and likely died there or close by, but that isn't a given. There are plenty of instances where the person was connected to the location for any number of reasons, but the common thread appears to be that they came into close proximity, if not fell victim to, death and the dying in that location.

To effectively clear that location, both the spirit and the origin of the disturbance must be dealt with. These are often the same thing, such as an object that contains the original imprint, or possibly a certain room at the site. More on this to come.

HOW TO RESPOND PHYSICALLY

Perform a level three cleansing (which includes a level one cleansing, remember?) and do the Positive Imprinting exercise on the location. It is an excellent idea to lean on the use of salt more at this stage, as it helps to provide immediate relief if you are feeling threatened by the energies present at the location.

Any person who lives in the space should undergo a thorough cleansing process that includes doing shadow work or therapy regarding any source of major stress in their lives. They should also take a series of salt baths, and increased spiritual security measures should be undertaken. Those personally affected by level four disturbances are at risk of causing a later resurgence and should take their physical and spiritual hygiene seriously.

EXERCISE TWENTY-SIX
Running Current

The following exercise is a useful tool when battling spirit attachments. It only works on people, and it should not be taken lightly. Though simple, the exercise uses a live running current of electricity to break etheric ties. To do this, procure a ten-foot extension cord and make a circle with it on the ground that is around three feet in diameter. Plug the cord into the socket and plug something like a lamp into the extension cord so that it is drawing current. Stand or sit in the center of the circle for five to ten minutes while you perform a personal grounding.

You can do this same exercise on a larger scale so that it encompasses a bed. This is particularly useful for people who feel watched or visited at night by spirits.

HOW TO RESPOND MENTALLY

As I have said since we started this journey, what spirit attachments want more than anything is your vital energy. When battling a level four disturbance, it is particularly important to keep an eye on your mood and state of mind. The attached spirit will likely do all it can to keep you occupied and distracted, often at your own expense. Mentally, the most important thing to do is to stay sober and focused on remaining present-minded. Watch for depression and anxiety, and do your best to avoid them at all costs.

HOW TO RESPOND SPIRITUALLY

There are two very famous and very important methods that we need to discuss now that likely have been misrepresented to you through movies and television. To respond spiritually to a level four disturbance, we likely will need to perform either a crossing-over or an exorcism, both have the same end result of getting the spiritual intelligence to leave. When performing these, there are some important ground rules to follow.

- You need to keep everything we have discussed up to this point in mind and you need to finish reading this book before you attempt to perform either one of these methods. You need to learn a bit more about using your abilities and protection.

- A crossing-over is a spiritual working that involves an assisted transcendence for the intelligence. This is where we get them to leave of their own accord after helping them understand what is happening to them. Often, spirits haunting a location are unaware of their condition or are confused, in which case a simple conversation and some energy work will do the trick.

- An eviction (aka exorcism) is a working wherein we muscle the psychic intelligence out of the thing or the person it is attached to via our own spiritual willpower, or our willpower with the assistance of a more aggressive spiritual power. Evictions are, generally speaking, though there are some exceptions, not voluntary on behalf of the spiritual intelligence. An eviction is essentially forcing the spirit in question to vacate the property, so to speak, and you should expect resistance.

- Getting physically aggressive with a spirit creates needless drama and could potentially put your life or someone else's life at risk. This work should be done with the intention of bringing peace to those affected, including the spirit, and stabilizing the spiritual ecosystem. Contrary to paranormal reality television, going postal when you are performing this kind of work is reckless and demonstrates a lack of personal development and spiritual prowess. The very last thing you want to do when you are crossing a spirit over or performing an exorcism is lose your cool. In reality, you want to be as unmovable as possible. You don't want to let the spiritual intelligence know you are excited by them.

EXERCISE TWENTY-SEVEN
Crossing a Spirit Over

How you go about crossing a spirit over is actually more dependent on the spirit's background than yours. Most people belong to a religion, and every religion has its own views of the afterlife. In order for a spirit to cross over, we have to use its/their own cultural and spiritual cues whenever possible. Only when we are without that awareness should we proceed with our own beliefs. Meaning, if you are crossing the spirit of a Jewish person over, you should at the very least find a prayer or some appropriate religious iconography, such as the Star of David. This clues the spirit into what is happening faster and helps them find peace quicker. Approaching them with a Mormon prayer would feel foreign and potentially abrasive to them.

When we are working with the spirits of the dead, we must remember that they are humans, and we should have all the considerations in mind with them as we would when working with a living person. Beyond that, remember that it isn't about you! It is about helping a person in their time of need.

If you are not particularly prone to speaking with spirits, then invite someone who is more adept at mediumship to join you for the process. If you don't have anyone who can help as a medium, work with tarot cards or oracle cards to act as the medium for you. Spirits love to use divination systems to communicate.

As a nonreligious type, if I am unable to find that spirit's religious context, I move on with a purely universal approach and speak in terms that (hopefully) transcend religious value and honor the divinity that remains inside that spirit.

Performing the working is easy on paper but more difficult in practice. First, you have to find the spirit in question. If it was a living person, you will need to figure out what their deal is, essentially. How they ended up there, what is keeping them there, and what it will take to get them to let go of their grip on this world. I find asking those questions directly to be the best approach. This is why you want someone with mediumship ability handy, if possible, as it makes the whole process move along much faster.

EXERCISE TWENTY-EIGHT
Bridge Reading

If you need to rely on tarot, here is a spread I developed to help discern the logistics.

Row Five:	17	18	19	20	21
Row Three:	1	4	13	7	10
Row Two:	2	5	14	8	11
Row One:	3	6	15	9	12
Row Four:					16

Draw twenty-one cards. Each row should be read as a collection of five cards (excluding the fourth row), and all cards should be considered important when divining.

Row one represents the physical properties surrounding the spirit's condition. This is where you will find information related to the way they died and what they remain connected to in the physical world.

Row two defines the condition of their current mental state. Here is where you will find information about what the spirit is focused on and its emotional background.

Row three defines the properties of their spiritual state, which is important for helping them to find peace and move on if they were a physical being. Here you will also find clues about any unfinished business they might have, as well as their fears regarding the afterlife.

Row four, which is just one card, provides information the spirit is hiding from you or has neglected to mention. I treat it like a wild card.

Row five provides information from that spirit's Higher Self, which is important to consider, as they often leave instructions for us. That person's Higher Self has likely moved on to another life and what remains in the form of the spirit or ghost is actually something more like a shed psychic skin. More on this to come.

Once you have gathered the info, call upon your spiritual support team and ask for their assistance. Much of the process from this point is simply in communicating with them and essentially being a bit of a counselor for the dead. Often, we find that what spirits want is for someone to sympathize with their suffering, someone to just look at them and say, "I see you. I am so sorry. You deserved better." It might sound silly, but compassion is the key to this whole process. Use the cards if you need to seek clarity, and take your time.

When they are ready, they will tell you. For me, this comes with a feeling of relief, of lifted sorrow. Like how you feel after a good cry but without the tears. When you feel that, or something akin to it, connect to Source and allow it pool into a ball over your head. Take three deep breaths, visualizing that ball getting brighter and brighter until it fills the space around you. Then, tell the spirit to step into the light. When you're done, disconnect from Source and do a level one cleansing on yourself.

EXERCISE TWENTY-NINE
Eviction

An exorcism is a religious ritual that is performed by a clergy person on a member of their flock who has become unwillingly possessed by a spiritual intelligence that is usually deemed to be antagonistic to their religion. For example, a Catholic priest exorcising a demon, as seen in movies and television. The process is fantasized by the media, as you might imagine, and it is all a lot more involved than we are led to believe.

Exorcisms are specific to the religion they belong to and are a tool of spiritual warfare often between two opposing forces. For the curious, you can easily find copies of various religious exorcisms all over the internet; however, if you aren't a member of the clergy, they won't do much good for you. Being a clergy person comes with certain blessings that are assumed to be vital to the process and without those an exorcism is not capable of working in most religions. As you might imagine, I cannot provide that type of information here. I can, however, provide an equally awesome and effective working that will get the job done.

An eviction is my way of taking care of matters and relies on universal laws of energy rather than religious thinking to expel a spiritual intelligence from a location or a person. It is a complex working in that, if evicting a spirit attachment from a person, the afflicted individual must be involved. If evicting from a location, those who live there must be involved.

At the heart of an effective eviction is that we are taking care of whatever led to the original disruption. This means that all parties involved must perform their own cleansing work and do any shadow work related to matters surrounding the disruption. This could mean the events leading up to it, surrounding it, or that happened after. Basically, we have to make sure that all individuals affected by the spirit are taken care of mentally, physically, and spiritually and that we are doing everything we can to treat the root cause of the attachment. The eviction will not work if those basic care steps aren't performed seriously.

You must have your entire spiritual security system working and in place when you do an exorcism. I explain all of this in the previous chapter. Again, you will want to read the whole book before trying this working. Only proceed when you are confident in your personal spiritual protection measures. Call upon your spiritual support team, including your Higher Self, and invite any spiritual figure heads that you work with, such as saint or angels.

As the person performing the eviction, your vital energies must be stable, and you must spend time restoring them after the working. In truth, the working is simple, the hard part is in being the dominant psychic force in the space and in taking each step in a calculated fashion. So, assuming you have your psychic security in check, and you have called upon your backup, proceed knowing that you are a badass sorcerer of divine light and that absolutely nothing can stop you now!

Begin the next step by becoming a beacon for Source energy. Think of yourself like a light bulb that is capable of becoming as bright as the sun at full potential. Perform the Channeling Source exercise, but instead of allowing the energy to flow through your hands, as I explain in part two of that exercise, allow it to fill up your entire body.

Breathe slow and deep, letting the light fill the spaces where you feel tension and simply be a vessel for Source energy. Fill yourself up until you are full and then allow the extra to emanate from you in all directions. Allow the energy that fills you to move beyond you and to enter the space.

Continue to breathe slow and deep, and push the light outward even farther, so that it fills every shadow and illuminates every crevasse. Spend a few moments maintaining this visualization and feeling what it is like to be a beacon for Source in this way. When you are able to maintain this sensation without giving it too much effort, proceed by locating the spirit.

Knowing where the spirit is located should be something you've already done by now. In the chance that it is playing hard to get, you will need to go room by room, shining your light, until you find it. The entity should have an immediate adverse reaction to your light once it comes in contact with it. Once you find it, stand in front of it. Instead of raising your voice, raise your vibration; increase the flow of Source you are emitting as radiant light by opening your psychic senses and dilating the access point at the top of your head. This is the psychic equivalent of fluffing your feathers.

Give the spiritual intelligence your demands. For me, this comes as an offer to help it cross over and a warning that I will take command of the situation if it does not leave of its own accord. Most of the time, even in these rare instances, this does the trick, and you can perform a crossing over. Spirits don't tend to want to argue with big balls of light.

If it doesn't leave on its own, then proceed without further warning. First, instruct your spirit allies to help you push the spirit out. Next, increase your light so that you shine as brightly as you possible can with Source energy. Push this energy outward so that it encases you and visualize yourself radiating at brightly as the sun. Recite the following mantra while you visualize the spiritual intelligence being absorbed by the light:

I shine with the light of the cosmos that knows no limitations. My will is made of this light, and it floods reality with my intention. My intention is to remove this spirit from this place. My mind shapes this reality and seizes all paradigms. This spirit has no footing here. My soul directs the flow of events in this reality and speaks with divine authority. Hear me now: flee this space or become one with the light. You are not welcome here.

Continue to shine brightly and to exert your spiritual dominance over the being by reciting "flee this space or become one with the light, you are not welcome here" over and over until you feel the spirit leave. Remember: don't raise your voice, raise your vibration. This might take some time, but remaining firm will eventually win you the battle. You will know it's over when you no longer feel resistance to the vital energies of Source that emit from your body. For me, this feels like breaking down a door.

When you are done, release your connection to Source above your head, and ground off any excess energy.

A few notes on this working. If you feel like the intelligence's vibration is too much to tackle on your own, call some real-life friends to help. Even I tend to travel with other experts to ensure success in these bigger cases. Perform a level three cleansing on the space and make sure all collected energy that remains from the disturbance is drained off properly. Finally, any personal details you have about the spirit should be used during the eviction. Meaning, if you know their name, then use it instead of saying "this spirit."

Evictions will work on all forms of spiritual intelligence if properly performed in accordance with the other measures mentioned here. They provide more of a holistic approach to the process of removing unwanted spiritual attachments.

LEVEL FIVE: SEVERE ATTACHMENTS AND HAUNTINGS

We are going to wrap up the scale by briefly discussing the last level of disturbance, which is identical to a level four disturbance, except the activity has become physically violent. This is the rarest of rares, but instances of disturbances growing so severe that they are capable of manifesting harm to those affected are well documented. This includes everything from spirit attachments that have drained their host dry to hauntings by intelligent spirits that have gotten too big for their own good. Severe hauntings and attachments are dangerous and require a delicate hand.

To treat a level five disturbance, do everything you would for a level four with the addition of backup in the form of a physical ally and your personal protections that need to be thoroughly established. If you are a religious person, you should call in the help of a clergy person. Because physical harm is a real concern, you will need to document any instances where someone gets hurt, and you should also travel with a first aid kit.

I wish I had some magic pill to fix these scenarios, but despite being well documented anecdotally, there isn't a whole lot of research about them. I have only experienced a small handful of instances where a spirit could push me or touch me, let alone wreak havoc. Still, I've seen enough to know that there are very real and very intimidating bad vibes out there with a mind of their own.

CONCLUSION AND JOURNALING

We took a tour through the final two levels of the Scale of Cleansing in this chapter and discussed several topics that are difficult to approach. Dealing with hauntings, poltergeists, and attachments is no easy task; it requires a show of force unlike any other. You can achieve relief from these things if you are willing to do the work and remain steadfast. Sometimes that work involves calling for backup and sometimes it takes more than a few tries. With perseverance and faith in your connection to the spiritual, you can tackle any vibe that comes your way, including those that go bump in the night.

Respond to the following prompts in your journal to further explore the material from this chapter.

1. What is the most unsettling thing in your opinion about the concept of a haunting? Why do you feel this way and

how do you feel this might potentially be a weakness when confronting a haunting?

2. What are three ways you can prepare yourself before you confront a spiritual entity?

3. What role do you think your spirit guides and other allies should play during a level four and five cleansing?

4. Who are spiritual allies that you can call upon other than your spirit guides to aide in a cleansing?

5. What are the crystals or plants that you might include as part of your cleansing. Why?

6. Hypothetically, if there were a sixth level to the scale, what would that look like? What vibes would it address?

(((PART FOUR)))

PROTECTION AND TRANSMUTATION

In my late twenties, I found myself with a book deal and a rapidly changing life. Suddenly I wasn't just some guy people found out about through obscure Google searches at three in the morning, I was at everyone's local bookstore and library waiting for them. Almost overnight, at least it felt that way at the time, I was getting a whole lot of attention and not all of it was good. Sure, there was the typical jealousy thing from peers who hadn't found their opportunity for success yet, but there were also strange and desperate people showing up at my job (I worked at a metaphysical store, so it could have been worse) and calling my relatives in an attempt to talk to me after I stopped responding to their emails.

All of this was happening while my father's health started to decline, my grandparents who I was close to were dying, and I found myself with a second and eventually third book contract. Needless to say, all of this resulted in me being thrown off-balance. Okay, it was more like being thrown overboard into the ocean and left to find my way back to shore. I didn't know it at the time, but I was suffering, and I couldn't even conceptualize the thought of spiritual balance. I was too busy just trying to make it to the end of each day without letting anyone down, including myself.

I was blind to how bad it was until I was invited to appear as a guest on television for the first time. The show was *ABC's To Tell the Truth,* which was a big deal. It was network television and a lot of people I knew were regular viewers. Everything was so hectic that I hadn't had the ability to prepare myself or to think about what putting myself out there even more would mean in the long-term.

Before I knew it, I was flying to Hollywood, and I found myself standing next to celebrities who I had been a fan of since I was a kid. I got to meet Alfonso Ribeiro from the *Fresh Prince of Bel Air*, Thomas Lennon from *Reno 911*, and even got to rub elbows with Cassandra Peterson, aka Elvira Mistress of the Dark. I should have been ecstatic, but I was exhausted and burnt out. I went back to my hotel after recording, ate the greasiest burger I have ever shoved in my mouth, and promised myself I was done for a while.

When I got home the next day, I instantly went back to the grind. I didn't really have a choice, and I told myself that I could manage. I went on like this for months until I had almost forgotten about Hollywood, and then the episode aired. Again, overnight I found myself the center of a lot of attention that

I wasn't prepared for, but this time it was on a scale I couldn't have imagined.

It turns out that I had been right about one thing: There are a lot more people dealing with the strange and unusual than most of us think. Unfortunately, I hadn't been taking care of myself, I hadn't fortified my spiritual anatomy, so when their eyes turned to me for help, there simply wasn't enough of me to go around. Answering questions, offering advice, and doing all the things I normally would felt almost painful. Realizing I had used up all of my energy, I surrendered to burnout and started the very long process of healing. It took years before I felt like I could jump back in 100 percent.

What became very clear in my recovery process was that my energetic and spiritual needs would shift as my life shifted. Doing the same set of exercises I had been doing prior to getting a book deal and going on television was not going to address the new types of vibes I would end up encountering. As I worked on my healing process, I leaned in on the concept of psychic protection in ways I hadn't before. I flipped what I thought I knew on its head and questioned everything. This allowed me to address the changes I needed to make and to find new techniques for how I approach the entire concept of spiritual protection altogether.

Ultimately, that is what I am asking you to do in this last part of the book. I want you to question what you have been doing for your own spiritual protection and ask if it is getting the job done for your current situation.

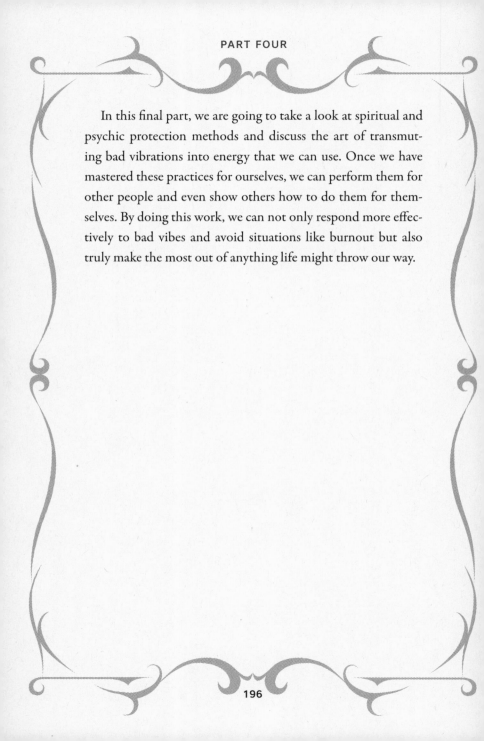

In this final part, we are going to take a look at spiritual and psychic protection methods and discuss the art of transmuting bad vibrations into energy that we can use. Once we have mastered these practices for ourselves, we can perform them for other people and even show others how to do them for themselves. By doing this work, we can not only respond more effectively to bad vibes and avoid situations like burnout but also truly make the most out of anything life might throw our way.

9

YOUR PERSONAL SECURITY SYSTEM

Psychic protection is a tricky thing, depending on who you are and where you come from. There are people who are just naturally more inclined to ward off unwanted vibrations and some, like me, have to learn how to navigate life being a magnet for them. When I first started my work, I was taught to shield myself as a means of protection from these things, but over the years I've learned that I needed something a little more on the potent side. In this chapter, I am going to do my very best to condense more than twenty years of hard-earned lessons into something practical and tangible that will hopefully save you time and energy.

Those who are developing a spiritual protection practice for the first time will find a clean and effective protocol that can be initiated in your life immediately. Those who already have a developed practice will find alternative methods for addressing often overlooked aspects of protection as well as an aggressive holistic approach that can easily be adjusted to suit your needs.

THINGS TO KEEP IN MIND

There are a million individual exercises out there for psychic protection, but not all of them are going to work for you. The reason is simple: there isn't a one-size-fits-all pattern for anyone to follow, though there have been plenty of attempts. What I have found to be true of myself and many others is that for us to find a good fit, we must tailor our practice to suit our lives and lifestyle. Like clothes, wearing something tailored to you is always going to be more comfortable than getting it off the rack.

IT'S ALL ABOUT WILLPOWER

Whether we are trying to keep ourselves safe from ambient bad vibes on a train or warding off a demonic spirit, it all boils down to a battle of willpower. I hate to simplify the matter to such a fine point. I almost feel bad for putting it all in those terms, but it's an unfortunate truth. When we perform cleansings, we are willing the vibration away, pushing it with our psychic senses. Now the task is to use our willpower to fabricate psychic armor capable of withstanding whatever may come, including direct attacks. Your willpower will ultimately be the substance your armor is made of, so doing things to help improve your willpower will be critical to long-term success. This means engaging in activities that both strengthen the mind as well as your personal resolve, even if those things aren't directly spiritual in nature, is essential for potency.

We are all a bit different, but our basic psychology is the same. Known ways to help increase willpower involve things like creating and sticking to routines, exercising, and self-affirmation, which can be game changers. Little things like getting enough sleep, meditating, and focusing on the moment can also go a long way in helping us to maintain our resolve. The key is to incorporate practices that help you manage stress and its effects on the mind, body, and spirit. Anything you can do that aids this process will be beneficial.

It is important to remember that when you are under attack from spiritual and psychic forces that your willpower itself will be a main target for negative energy, especially those connected to a form of consciousness. The opposite of willpower is weakness, and that is exactly what the bad vibes want. They want you weak so you're easily manipulated, and they can farm you for more energy.

IT IS OKAY TO ASK FOR HELP

All the pros ask for help. While it is true that it's a battle of wills out there, it is important to remember that willpower is accumulative. You can ask other people (living or otherwise) to help by lending some of their own willpower to your cause. You can elicit the support of known psychic energy producers such as plants and stones; this is essentially what shamans, witches, and mystics do. Regardless of your personal spiritual background, there is always someone or something that can help. We will talk more about this later in the chapter.

BE PRESENT-MINDED AND KNOW
YOUR LIABILITIES AND SOFT SPOTS

The most effective way to protect ourselves from bad vibes is to avoid them and to be prepared for them when they do inevitably come our way. This means we have to be present-minded, just like warriors in battle, and focused on our surroundings and the things that matter most to us. Those things that we care about and feel need protection are, for lack of a better term, liabilities in battle. For me, this means avoid battle at all costs, but it is nevertheless an aspect of the whole picture we cannot overlook because they make us vulnerable. For you to be properly protected, your efforts must include the protection of your liabilities.

This will likely mean that you have to develop a multipronged approach that includes dedicated time and attention devoted to the well-being of your liabilities. If you aren't sure what your liabilities are, think of your anchors, your home, your career, and your community. Those are usually where our liabilities tend to come from.

THINK SECURITY SYSTEM, NOT JUST ARMOR

You are far more complex than you might realize, and you'll need to think big if you want to develop long-term solutions that will cover you and your liabilities. The key is to ensure that protections are in place on all three levels of being (MBS) and that you allow them to evolve over time to suit your needs. The sky is the limit, and it's a good idea to play around with different techniques when creating your system. What works wonders for me might not work for you and over time our needs change. Having a system that can be augmented when you find a new technique is far superior to starting all over again. Building a quality security system also allows us to be protected in multiple ways, providing redundancies and firewalls so that even if something makes it past our front lines of defense, we are still covered.

ONCE YOU GET GOING, THINGS MIGHT GET WEIRD

It shouldn't surprise you by now when I say that bad vibes are going to get their feathers in a ruffle when you start throwing up effective spiritual protections. You will likely encounter a bit of a temper-tantrum from negativity in your life when you begin the work we discuss in this chapter. That's okay! Hunker down, batten down the hatches, and ride out the storm. Take this sudden upheaval as a sign that you have done something meaningful and important and cleanse, cleanse, cleanse!

YOU MUST STAY CLEAN

Over half of the work involved in creating your own spiritual security system is going to be in maintaining your overall spiritual health. The more you stay focused on living bad-vibe free, the less bad vibes you are going to run into that might cause potential issues. That doesn't mean you shouldn't be dealing with issues, quite the contrary, it means you should be making a concerted effort to keep things in balance, to seek out spiritual harmony, and to regularly cleanse your spiritual body.

Much of the bad vibes we face could have been nipped in the bud had they been cleansed early on. Having a psychic/spiritual hygiene regimen that includes a weekly level one cleansing at bare minimum is the best way to deter potential issues. Additionally, as stated elsewhere, work on yourself, heal your spirit from the past, and orient your thoughts to a future unbridled by negativity (regardless of where it comes from).

THE MIND-BODY-SPIRIT CONNECTION IS KEY

The last little bit to remember before we go on is that an effective security system is a holistic security system. Just as we would respond to and treat bad vibes from a mind, body, and spirit perspective, we need to prepare for them in a similar manner. All three aspects of ourselves are also the parts that are the most exposed to bad vibes, each possessing their own vulnerabilities. When they are each given consideration and empowered for protection, those vulnerabilities are less exposed and better hidden. As part of your efforts to create a spiritually protected life, be sure to do things that nurture each of those aspects of yourself.

INSTALLING YOUR SECURITY SYSTEM

Let's face it, having a spiritual practice is fantastic, when you can find the time and energy to do it. Being less spiritually active doesn't make you a bad person or a less worthy individual of protection. I have had strange conversations with folks who seem to think that a lapse in their practice, or a temporary disruption to their spiritual progress, somehow equates to them being less valuable in the eyes of the spiritual. That simply isn't true.

No matter the intensity and depth of your spiritual connection to the Universe, it has a vested interest in you. And by Universe, of course, I am talking about whoever or whatever made us. I don't really care to define it, but I know it wants us all healthy and safe. So that all being said, you deserve to be spiritually protected no matter who you are or where you come from, regardless of how much time you put into your spiritual journey in this life. You matter and you are capable of whatever you put your mind and soul to. Remember this as we move along.

Assuming that you are doing the cleansing and shadow work that we've talked about, the process of installing your spiritual security system is actually quite simple because you already have one! All we need to do is make sure it is in proper working order, and you are already doing most of that heavy lifting with your regular spiritual hygiene regimen. From here on out, unless you are facing a specific concern, the focus is going to be on how you are projecting and programing your vital energies. If something specific comes up, these protections should be enough to keep you in a place of power when confronting them and the previous chapter will give you the specifics for how to address them. For now, let's draw our attention to further developing our projective psychic abilities.

To build the security system, we are going to need to create a series of spiritual and mental tools that we can rely upon over and over again within a split second of needing them. To do this, we have to repeat these processes multiple times until they become second nature to us. We refer to this process as "programming," which is not entirely different from programming a stone or a crystal ally. By programming ourselves to respond in a certain way, we can skip a lot of chaotic decision-making and distracting thoughts that get in the way when all we really need is to be protected. Doing this will not only help you to deal with things in the moment but this repetition will also give your psychic and spiritual muscles a workout, helping you to become and remain spiritually fit.

We are going to approach this process through a series of guided meditations and energy exercises. Follow along, visualize the exercises as I describe them, and then revisit them on your own after. You won't always need to do the initial steps of each process, in fact you will likely develop shortcuts, but it is highly encouraged that you revisit the way they are written from time to time, if only to ensure proper technique.

PART ONE: THE INNER TEMPLE/PANIC ROOM

At the heart of our security system lies the panic room, a space so secure that nothing external from you can enter it without your expressed permission. This is the place where you will go when you feel depleted or like you are under attack. It is also going to function as a sort of command center from which all other aspects of our security system will stem from. Think of it as both your fortress of solitude and your control room.

EXERCISE THIRTY
Building the Inner Temple

This place must exist in your mind, if nowhere else, as it is through your visualization that it can become real in the metaphysical. Sit quietly in meditation and visualize an empty room and fill it up with whatever you want, or you can anchor it in something more physical, like an actual sanctuary space that you are familiar with. The main idea here is that you create a little space to operate from, a temple where you are both god and priest, a palace in your mind that only you have access to. Yep, we are building a mind palace!

In the interest of summarizing what could be thought of as an incredibly boring exposition, mind palaces (aka memory palaces) are used as a memorization strategy to help recall detailed information. The process has been hacked by the spiritual community to help bring order to chaos, though the roots of the technique are present in several shamanic traditions.

It might help to later get out some paper and draw the dimensions of the space or to sketch details that you can remember. Get creative and construct the sanctuary of your dreams. Keep it simple so that it will be easy to recall. Avoid confusing details that won't be immediately available when you think of the space. You can always go back and update it later, so for now focus on imagining a place where you have total peace and total control.

At the very center of the space, place a statue of yourself or some sort of image. This isn't to idolize yourself in secret with, though if that is your trip, go for it. We are placing this here so you have a representation of yourself to look at that will show you the current state of your vital energies. Think of this representation as a real-time replica of your current spiritual state. When it is clean and vibrant, you are in peak condition; when you notice it fade, become dingy, or anything that diminishes it, you can take that as a sign that there is work to do. The dirtier it gets, the worse off the situation.

The last thing you need to do here is create a place where you can be shown images, such as a reflecting pond, a mirror, or a monitor. Here you will let your spiritual senses show you things that you otherwise cannot see in the physical world. You will also want a dedicated space where you can meet with your spirit guides. Once you have the image of yourself, the imaging surface, and the meeting space installed, you are done with the hard part of the exercise.

Spend at least five minutes in the morning and in the evening each day for the next week visiting this space and recalling those details. Use that time to actually check in with your guides, check in on the image, and see if there is anything on the imaging surface. You can move on with installing your security system after you build the panic room, just be sure to finish the remaining visits over the following week.

PART TWO: SECURE YOUR VITAL FORCES

The next part of the process is to put up a series of barriers between you and the potential bad vibes that are out there. It is important to note that energy you produce inside these barriers will remain with you, because when we do this, we aren't just putting up a wall, we are also creating a container. You should consider these walls so strong that nothing can get in or out without your expressed permission. This is also one of the reasons why regular cleansing is important, as it provides one of the only opportunities for you to flush your system out. There will be others, and we will discuss alternative ways to handle the energy you produce inside this space, but for now simply focus on building impenetrable barriers as we move along.

Part two is still all about you. However, much of what we do at this stage will also come in handy when we start extending our protection out toward our environment and other people.

We are going to work with your existing energy body to establish three unique lines of defense that are responsible for the security of your vital bodies. Each of these is going to have a special job that it does, and each is tied directly back to your inner temple. This part will employ our core beliefs to help program the energy as we go along.

EXERCISE THIRTY-ONE
The Inner Protective Layer

For this exercise, I want you to recall the work we did all the way back in the first chapter regarding the channeling of Source energy. Source energy is pure and untainted, it can be manipulated into just about anything given the right conditions, and it is particularly resistant to corruption.

Ground and center yourself and perform the Pouring and Directing Flows of Source exercise from chapter 1. Instead of pooling the energy inside of your solar plexus, I would like you to collect it into a sphere shape over your head. As you visualize the iridescent energy forming above you, reach out with your spiritual senses for your Higher Self and claim your spiritual authority by reciting Core Belief Set One. Here it is one more time, so you don't have to look back:

> **I am safe and protected. I am worthy and loved.**
> **I am in control of my mind, body, and soul.**
> **My spirit is wise; it knows what to do.**
> **My vibration is strong; it overrides all others.**
> **My intention is clear; it takes precedent over my**
> **fear. I am capable. I am powerful. I am in control.**

As you recite the core belief, feel the words resonate through your entire being. When you feel ready, visualize the sphere cracking open like an egg, releasing the Source energy like a thick honey that pours over you. Notice that it only sticks to you, that it is attracted only to you, and that as it envelops you that it begins to harden. Take three deep breaths, allowing the energy to settle into a thin and impermeable layer that acts like a second skin. Recite Core Belief Set One out loud, and as you do this, visualize yourself glowing outward with the brilliance of hardened Source energy.

This barrier serves to protect your Higher Self and your vital energies.

EXERCISE THIRTY-TWO
The Middle Intermediary Layer

Perform the previous exercise exactly as stated, grounding and centering yourself and collecting a sphere of Source energy above your head. Instead of reciting the first core belief, recite the second, and visualize the energy above you turning into a solid black that is so deep it is the color of outer space. Black is a powerfully protective color, known for absorbing all light. Notice, however, that even though the energy has turned to the color of space, it still emits the same iridescent glow somehow.

Core Belief Set Two is:

> My mind, body, and soul move as one being. What I think and feel become physical through my being. My being gives me power in all worlds, authority over all unwelcome vibrations, and is undeniable.

As you recite the core belief, feel the words resonate through your entire being. When ready, visualize the sphere cracking open as before, releasing the Source energy like a thick honey that pours over you. Notice that it only sticks to you, that it is attracted only to you. As it envelops you, it begins to harden. As it does this, it encapsulates the first layer, acting as your second line of defense. Take three deep breaths, allowing the energy to settle into a thin and impermeable layer that acts like a second skin. Recite the first core belief again out loud and as you do this, visualize yourself glowing outward with the brilliance of hardened Source energy but also notice that this second barrier hides your personal features.

This barrier serves to protect your etheric anatomy, which are essentially your spiritual organs. The mind, body, and soul are the three largest organs in this system, but you can break this system down into further distinct parts, such as the chakras. This will stop psychic vampires and energy attachments from latching on.

EXERCISE THIRTY-THREE
The Outer Protective Layer

Okay, this time we are going to do exactly the same thing, but we are going to recite the third and fourth sets of core beliefs and visualize the energy pouring down as reflective paint. When it hardens, visualize your figure as a mirror that reflects everything back out in all directions.

CORE BELIEF SET THREE

I am stronger than fear. Fear is a weapon my enemy uses to intimidate and take my power. I will not give my enemy this weapon. I will not concede to fear.

CORE BELIEF SET FOUR

I am unquestionably divine, and my divinity gives me authority in this world and in others.

This barrier serves as your last layer of personal armor and will reflect incoming bad vibes that are floating out there in general. This is the layer I reinforce the most, meaning I go back and refresh this layer as part of my regular spiritual work.

Just like with the first part, revisit this exercise twice a day for about a week. However, perform it while visualizing yourself in front of the image of you in your mind palace. Visualize the different layers also manifesting on the image.

PART THREE: SECURE THE PERIMETER

Now we will begin the process of extending our energy outward to protect our homes, loved ones, and even belongings. We've done the work of identifying what our liabilities and soft spots are and here is where we can make sure that those elements of our lives are taken care of!

I think the important thing to remember is that you cannot be in all places at once, and you can't always stop what you are doing to check in with your security system. Furthermore, speaking from personal experience, you cannot be the sole provider of energy to your security system. To make this work, we need to incorporate vital energies that are not our own, that can do their thing without us directing their flow in real time. This includes incorporating plants, minerals, and other third parties. We can use bad vibes that are sent to us or that we pick up on accident as fuel for our security system.

To me, this is the fun part! I enjoy getting creative with how I incorporate psychic protections into my life, and I hope you do, as well. This is also where your personality gets to shine through and where we can really open to our spiritual allies for inspiration.

WORKING WITH YOUR GUIDES FOR PROTECTION

The first act of securing the perimeter is to make sure you've hired a security guard, or in our case, brought your spirit guide on as a full-time member of staff. Our guides not only have a lot to share with us about our spiritual journey but they can also teach us unique methods for cleansing, protection, and transmutation.

Your spirit guides and allies that are connected to your highest good, aka your spiritual support team, are heavily invested in your protection. In reality, they are protecting you all the time, in some religious traditions they are called "guardian angels," after all. The number one cause of us not feeling like they are doing their job or like we don't feel their presence with us, is that we aren't actually taking the time to listen to them.

Developing mediumship of any kind is all about learning to listen. Before we can do that, however, we have to set time and space aside for this to happen. It took a long time for me to realize that there are the everyday messages that come through my spirit team, but there are also many messages that are just too complex to receive through simply passing it along when my mind is otherwise occupied. These messages only come through when I dedicate time to receiving them in their entirety.

We already made sure this wouldn't be a problem by creating a space just for them in our inner temple where we can meet. We also have the original meeting place that was introduced in the first chapter. Your guides will be part of your advanced warning system, but only if you let them!

Check in with them on a regular basis, ask them for information if you feel like bad vibes are afoot, but most importantly, use your check-ins as an excuse to further your relationship with them. Just like any friendship, the more time you devote to getting to know one another, the deeper those bonds will grow.

THE SECURITY GUARD (OPTIONAL)

Our spirit guides work to protect us, and if we let them, they do a damn fine job at it. Those of us who find ourselves dealing with a lot of heavy energy, emotional energy, or psychic energy as part of life might need to call in extra backup. For example, it is in my experience that folks who work in the preternatural or paranormal tend to need as much extra protection as possible. First responders and those who work in hospitals and nursing homes often need a little extra. There are two ways to do this: ask for a recommendation from your spirit guides or create a thoughtform. Either way, it never hurts to have a full-time security guard patrolling your network.

EXERCISE THIRTY-FOUR
Getting a Recommendation from Your Guide

If we ask our spirit guides if they need help or have recommendations for allies who could help, they respond quickly and often help us find other spirits to join our cause. The allies they recommend are often in alignment with who they are, which means they are going to be in alignment with you. Go to the meeting room in your inner temple and discuss security tactics with your guide(s). Ask them to introduce you the following day to a compatible spirit who you can work with on a regular basis.

Just like in the exercise where we met our guides for the first time, you want to ask for the help, leave, and then come back the next day. We need time for the inner temple to reset, and we need to allow them time to bring their friend. Go back the next day and they should be there. Go through the same process of vetting them out as you did in the first exercise of Meeting Your Guides.

EXERCISE THIRTY-FIVE
Creating an Intentional Thoughtform

This is my preferred method, as it allows for the most control; however, it is definitely on the advanced side of psychic and spiritual development. Unlike spirits guides, which have their own personality and their own way of going about things, a thoughtform is restricted to a predetermined range of motion. If you create a thoughtform for protection, it will only do what you ask it to. Over time, it will grow stronger and will develop a personality, which has been a lot of fun to behold in my personal experience, but it will always remain tethered to you and, ultimately, will be an extension of your vital forces.

Creating an intentional thoughtform takes time, but the concept is simple if you are familiar with the basics of energy, philosophy, and mediumship. There are, of course, a lot of ways to go about this, but for our purposes, we are going to focus on creating a thoughtform specifically to act as a bodyguard.

STEP ONE: SEED THOUGHT/BELIEF

Like a core belief, this seed thought is going to contain the vital message that our thoughtform will grow from. For our working, we are going to use the phrase, "*(Insert name here)* is spiritually protected from all harm and undesirable energy." Look at yourself in the mirror and say it out loud as if it were a matter of fact five times.

STEP TWO: CREATE AN IMAGE

Think of a protective animal that you'd like this thoughtform to take the shape of when you interact with it. For this example, let's use a rottweiler dog. Draw the creature if it helps to visualize it. Go to your inner temple and see the animal waiting for you.

Call out to it, using the seed thought as its name. Yeah, I know "*(Insert name here)* is spiritually protected from all harm and undesirable energy" is a long name, but you will shorten it later. The important thing is to implant the seed thought immediately so that it becomes its identity. Let the creature respond by lovingly coming to you for affection, and praise it for being a good thoughtform, using the name again at least two more times. When you feel a connection establish between the two of you, give it a nickname.

STEP THREE: PROGRAM THE THOUGHTFORM

Once you feel connected to it, give it detailed instructions on how you would like it to perform for you. Your spirit guide might have a few suggestions here, so be sure to ask! For me, I find keeping it simple is the best way to go, and I program my thoughtforms to eat the bad vibes they encounter and transmute the energy into something that can be used to reinforce the protections already in place.

STEP FOUR: LET IT GROW!

This will take time, but the more you engage with the thoughtform, the better. I treat mine like invisible pets, rewarding them for jobs well done with music that I associate with them and talk to them as if they were in the room with me. I find that doing this is the fastest way to get them to grow. Do this daily and do not tell anyone about them until you feel them well established.

As part of maintaining the network, you will want to hold regular meetings with your security guard. The only drawback to this is that when you get an ally to perform in this role for you, you end up with another thing to take care of and maintain. That isn't always ideal for everyone. While I find my security guards to be invaluable, I also can see how the average spiritual person wouldn't need this degree of protection.

WORKING WITH PLANT ALLIES
FOR PROTECTION

Speaking of growing, have you heard about the amazing spiritual protection that comes from the plant kingdom? Nature is full of friends that want us to live happy, healthy lives, and some green allies are particularly suited for helping us in the art of spiritual defense.

If your perimeter includes a space that includes established plants and/or trees, one of the best practices you can develop is to connect with them and simply directing them to help with the energetic maintenance of the property. They do this on their own, but if there are specific concerns, definitely bring that to their attention. Trees are great at helping to anchor energy down and are natural focal points for energy within an environment. Go outside, put your hand on the oldest tree you find, and simply ask it for protection. I know it sounds utterly absurd, but there is an intelligence in all plants, and they do listen.

I have become accustomed to working with houseplants for this purpose and there are a lot of great options available for those who are able to grow them. Not only do most of them help to purify the air, which in turn purifies the energy within the environment, but several also have the propensity to act as psychic muscle for hire. In exchange for proper care, they will keep bad vibes from coming into the home or developing within it. For more information about this and different methods to explore with houseplants in your spiritual journey, check out my book (shameless plug) *Houseplant Hortocculture*!

In reality, the frequencies put off by the plants I am about to recommend aren't all about protecting the space because they love you and want you to be surrounded with good vibes. What makes them so great to work with is that their energies are dominating and territorial, even if they themselves are small and sitting on a windowsill. The following houseplants are easy to take care of, have a wide range of influence in the home, and are presented to you in no particular order.

SANSEVIERIA

These are sometimes called mother-in-law's tongue but most often are known simply as snake plants. These are hard to kill and come in a large range of forms. Most notably, they grow in clusters of swordlike leaves that jet out from the substrate and are known for their thickness. These are especially great to have near entrances as guardians for the household.

ZAMIOCULCAS ZAMIFOLIA

Also known as the ZZ plant, there is a limited spectrum to their variety, however they range from black to yellow, most being a vibrant green. Their tough, leathery leaves are shaped like blades and protrude from a central stock. Placing these in high traffic areas helps to break energies apart and prevents energies that are inharmonious from settling.

MONSTERA DELICIOSA

Monsteras, regardless of the variety, are particularly suited to the cause of protection. This is especially true of the *Monstera deliciosa*, which has massive leaves when mature that provide ample coverage in the wild. They are another hard to kill species and, in my experience, love to be worked with to shield against unwanted psychic attacks.

EPIPREMNUM

Also called pothos, *Epipremnum* is a very common houseplant that you can find in most grocery stores these days. Also known as devil's ivy because it can grow prolifically, its fast nature is truly something to behold. The real protection energies come from its ability to spread out and cover a large area if allowed. Use that to your advantage when working with them. These are good for protecting against most energies out there, but I find them best suited for emotional vampirism and attachments.

CACTI

The last plant I am going to recommend is the humble cactus. There are thousands of options when it comes to the cacti family, and you can find some variety of them at any hardware store. Cacti are hardy but sensitive to overwatering. As you might imagine, their thorny spines make them ideal protection allies. I have them all over my house as general wards, as they are good for protecting our space from any unwanted outside vibes.

OTHER PLANT METHODS TO CONSIDER

While adding houseplants will make an immediate change on your environment, it is also going to take a few weeks for the effects to fully kick in. If you are looking for something simpler and likely to work quickly, you can always use dry herb blends that are sprinkled, placed in sachets or bowls, or folded into prayer papers that are distributed around the property. Dried herbs obviously pair with salt easily too.

Burning herbs as incense is another way to work with plants for protection, though do make sure you aren't allergic to what you are working with, especially before you burn it. On the other side of the spectrum, we have teas and baths, which help us to draw out the essence of the plant into water. Herbs such as bay leaves, rosemary, lavender, and sage are easily found in grocery stores and can be blended or used individually in both baths and incense. Also, if you are making incense, add a bit of copal, dragon's blood, or frankincense resin to take both the scent and the working to a whole new level.

WORKING WITH CRYSTAL ALLIES
FOR PROTECTION

The mineral kingdom is loaded with allies that make fantastic cohorts when seeking protection, and they each transmute spiritual energy in their own way. In truth, just about every mineral can be worked with for protection in one way or another and I don't think that is by accident. Chances are, your favorite crystal or mineral is your favorite because it protects you in some way, or you are instinctively drawn to the protective qualities that it possesses. It isn't always about going out and buying a shiny rock, though.

The best place to look when partnering with the mineral kingdom for protection is to connect directly to the natural rocks and unique geology of the place where you live or are working to protect. Here in the United States, we have ample deposits of limestone and shale, both of which are loaded with protective qualities. If you live in a region where there is or was volcanic activity, the chances of having variations of obsidian local to you are high. There are also deposits of other semi-precious and precious minerals scattered all throughout the world, and the chances of your region being known for at least one is relatively high, as well. Start local and build a connection with what is already there.

When it comes to shiny rocks that you can work with, I have a whole list of go-tos. I find the mineral kingdom to be particularly easy to work with for protection. There are a few schools of thought about how to go about picking a stone that might be a good fit for you and your needs. My main go-to is to follow your gut, always, but not all of us have access to a crystal showroom where you can play with a bunch of rocks before you buy them. There are a handful of stones that I always find myself recommending for their ease of use and accessibility.

Black stones such as tourmaline, obsidian, onyx, and shungite are all famous for their protective qualities. Hematite contains heavy amounts of iron, and bloodstone has iron present as well, both of which are easy to find.

When in doubt, go for good ol' iron! I have grown accustomed to working with chunks of iron ore that I grabbed off an internet auction site for cheap. I also keep a stash of railroad spikes handy, which are made from iron and are used in the laying of railroad tracks. Again, another online find. Placing iron at the compass points in the home and at the entrances will help to drain off energy and keep it from accumulating, but it also helps to provide a nearly impenetrable area of influence.

You can wear stones as jewelry or carry them in your pocket. It is not advised, as a general rule of thumb, to wear iron for extended periods of time, as it will weaken your vital energies like any other form of energy.

OTHER TOKENS OF PERSONAL POWER

I think it is worth noting that items that are special to us are also loaded with energy. You may have one or two things in your possession right now that would make excellent partners as you build your security system. For example, I have an old hat perched near the door of my studio that my grandfather used to wear. It isn't so much that I have it there to keep my grandfather's spirit close, but more so the spirit of what he meant to me. Time with him was always good and happy, I felt safe and secure. Placing the hat there channels that feeling of security into my space and helps to fill my environment with protection. Look around your life for special tokens of personal power and incorporate them into your surroundings.

ESTABLISHING YOUR NETWORK

Now that we have talked about allies you can bring into your space to help with the heavy lifting, let's dive in to how to put these all together.

As you place these plants, crystals, or tokens of personal power around your space, do so with intention by giving them clear verbal instruction. If you haven't felt silly yet, just wait until you are verbally instructing a houseplant to keep your neighbor's bad vibes from coming into your home! I think the verbalization is important in that it helps to create space for them as real articles of spiritual potency.

Play with where you put things and explore the intentional use of space. When you feel like you've created the right type of environment, look around and take a mental note of where things are and why you placed them as you did. We will get back to this in just a moment.

Your network not only includes your living space (or any space you are protecting) but also the people and things that have an immediate impact on you. Take a few moments to write out who or what those are and keep this list next to you. My advice is to start with three or four and then add when your protection work is better established.

EXERCISE THIRTY-SIX
Programming the Security Network

Go to your inner temple/panic room and visualize a map of your environment on the imaging surface you built that shows where you've placed any intentional protection items. Go through them one by one and touch their place on the map. As you do this, visualize a jolt of energy leave your finger, travel through the screen, and connect to that item, making a pure line of psychic energy. Do this for each item.

Next, on your imaging surface visualize the people or items you wish to be protected by your network. Take a series of grounding breaths, then see a sphere of Source energy surround them. Touch the screen as before, sending a jolt of Source to them, and establish a connection to them.

Allow yourself to spend as much time reviewing the map as possible before ending the exercise. Then, check in on your spirit guide and security guard. Revisit and perform this exercise again to reestablish links if you feel the connection weakening. Visit the map as often as you need when you want to check in on your security system.

PART FOUR: ACTIVATING
THE SECURITY SYSTEM

The final act that will tie it all together comes as we activate our personal security system and raise the outermost barrier. From here on out, once you've done this exercise all you should ever need to do to maintain the work done is to visit your inner temple and to check in on a regular basis. When you feel elements of it weaken or if they seem to fade away, perform the part of the working that relates to them.

EXERCISE THIRTY-SEVEN
Shields Up!

Go to the imaging surface inside your inner temple and recall the map of your network. Check in with the different elements, touching the map and sending a jolt of power to keep them strong as you've done before. Take a few deep breaths, and draw upon Source energy, allowing it to pool into a sphere at the center of your chest at your solar plexus. Take a series of three deep breaths, allowing the sphere to grow large each time, until it fully encompasses you. Recite the first set of core beliefs aloud. They are:

> I am safe and protected. I am worthy and loved.
> I am in control of my mind, body, and soul. My
> spirit is wise; it knows what to do. My vibration
> is strong; it overrides all others. My intention
> is clear; it takes precedent over my fear. I
> am capable. I am powerful. I am in control.

In response to the core belief, see the Source energy form into a membrane, as if you were standing inside of a giant inflated balloon with thick walls. See that this psychic membrane is not solid, but rather permeable and responds to stimuli. Through it spiritual messages, inspiration, and all the good stuff can flow, but it will act like a filter for the rest.

Take another series of deep breaths and push the sphere outward in all directions, stretching until it encompasses the immediate surroundings on the map. Then, extend through the lines of energy outward to those other elements of your network. As the light moves through and touches them, see them light up on the map, and then bring your attention back to the sphere's expansion.

When you are finished, sit for a few moments and reach out to feel the barrier from the inside. Familiarize yourself with the look and feel of this state and then open your eyes. The work is done.

CONCLUSION AND JOURNALING

You are important and you are worthy of security. There are no ifs, ands, or buts about it. When it comes to protecting ourselves spiritually, it is easy to get overwhelmed or to even get bamboozled by frauds promising to fix everything with a chant and a reading. True spiritual protection comes from doing the hard work of healing ourselves and empowering our weaknesses. From that growth we can build a strong outer shell, or in our case, a security system, that is capable of responding to bad vibes in real time, without the need for constant maintenance.

Even if you only take a few of the exercises or concepts from this chapter and incorporate them into your practice, you will notice a marked degree of improvement. If you can go all out and set up the whole network, you will be in better shape to deal with the rigors of life in the spirit world. To help take what we discussed here further, respond to the following prompts in your journal.

1. After reading through this chapter, which exercises stuck out to you as being valuable to you? Why?

2. Which of the methods that we discussed here, if any, are you not interested in trying? Why?

3. Identify areas in your life that you feel particularly vulnerable about and how your security system can address them.

10

TRANSMUTATION AND REFORMATTING VIBES

Spiritual transmutation is the art of taking one psychic substance and turning it into another. This is something most of us don't come across in many books on the psychic and spiritual because its generally considered to be an advanced practice and is one of those things we usually have to get a teacher for. I don't think there is anything to gatekeep here. I learned of it through my esoteric studies. However, it isn't the easiest thing to do, especially if you don't sense psychic energy well.

A big requirement for transmutation to work is that you are capable of spiritually sensing subtle shifts, and that isn't everyone's cup of tea. If you have been following along and have had success with the exercises in this book, I'm willing to bet you can transmute energy as well.

Beginners might find this chapter a bit of a struggle, but if they are adventurous, they will find adding transmutation early in their development will bring them ahead of the curve compared to the normal progression of skill. The practice will help them to develop insights about energy that would otherwise take a potential lifetime to unearth. Readers who are intermediate and advanced will find the topics and exercises in this chapter a worthwhile challenge that will help them to beef up their existing practice and skills.

Part of what makes transmutation difficult is that there is a lot of experimentation that we have to do. It is a form of spiritual alchemy and every formula or process that we explore will need to be adjusted to meet the specific demands of the transmutation. It isn't as simple as just flipping a switch; we have to use all of our skills to guide the process along. Unlike our security system, where we can set it up to largely run itself, transmutation requires vigilant oversight and tinkering. In this chapter, we are going to take a look at three unique methods for transmuting energy, going from slow and simple to rapid and complex.

The end goal for all transmutations is to take the bad and turn it into something positive and useful. We can use the energy rendered from the process to fuel our security system, to heal ourselves, or to help restore an area that is afflicted by one form of bad vibration or another. The options are endless, really. What matters is that you direct it into a meaningful cause, otherwise what's the point?

SAFETY FIRST

Before we dive into the methods, I want to go over the risks involved with transmutation, of which there aren't many. One of the other reasons this is advanced stuff is that you have to be able to deal with the bad vibes if you fail to transmute them. They don't just vanish. If the bad vibe involves a spirit of any kind, you might just piss it off. (Ask me how I know from personal experience next time you see me.) For your own spiritual safety and that of those in your immediate sphere, make sure you are well protected and that you have the ability to quickly adjust plans, or even remove the vibration altogether if something should go wrong when working with the two methods covered in this chapter.

METHOD ONE:
HYDRO TRANSMUTATION

This is one of the exercises that I started my transmutation work with, and unlike the others, there isn't any risk of something going wonky with it. You simply get more proficient at it over time. If you include it as part of your regular routine, it can be a personal transmutation technique that can move mountains of spiritual energy.

It was first introduced to me as Kala or, the Waters of Purity, by my partner Storm Faerywolf, and it is one of the easiest metaphysical techniques I have ever learned. All you need to get started is a glass of water and a few minutes without distraction. You don't even need to know what you are going to be transmuting ahead of time, though having an idea can be quite useful.

EXERCISE THIRTY-EIGHT
Hydro Transmutation

Sitting or standing, it doesn't matter, take a few minutes to check in with your mind, body, and spirit. Tune in to the different parts of your being, and once you feel each of those pieces individually, allow them to become one working system in your mind's eye. See the mind, body, and spirit as a unified presence and closed circuit. Take a few moments to scan the circuit, checking for anything that might be attached or stuck to your spiritual body. Normally we would cleanse these things, but they are exactly what we need for this practice. You might not be able to conceptualize the vibes, they could be a feeling or a picture, whatever they are and however they present themselves in your energy body, simply observe.

Pick up the glass of water and hold it at heart level. Take three deep breaths, exhaling over the surface of the water. As you do this, visualize the unwanted energy inside your circuit being swept up with each inhale and released into the water as you exhale. As it leaves you and enters the water, visualize the water growing thick and oily, perhaps even heavy with the vibration.

Next, perform the exercise Focusing and Connecting to Source from chapter 1. Direct Source energy into the water, giving it the mental command to transmute the unwanted energy it contains into pure Source. Take another three breaths, this time visualizing the water becoming lighter with each exhale, until it is glowing with Source on the final breath. Discontinue channeling and immediately drink the water.

Finally, visualize the Source energy moving down into your gut and being absorbed wholly by the physical body, bringing nourishing energy to every part of your physical, mental, and spiritual being.

METHOD TWO: AMBIENT TRANSMUTATION

This method of transmutation is the simplest because it models itself after the cycles observed in nature. We have already discussed ley lines, which are a natural system of energetic veins and arteries that move through our planet. This system demonstrates Earth's transmutation process and can be used as a template for how we might go about this process as well.

I refer to this as ambient because the transmutation occurs through a simple filtration system that is distributed throughout the environment and mimics the function of ley lines. They work to transmute energy through ambient channels and can easily be made part of your spiritual security system. This method works best for homes and other physical locations and is nicely suited to dealing with everyday bad vibes.

As you grow more confident with this method, you can make it more complicated, but for this introduction, select one specific vibration that you would like to transmute. You also need to decide on something simple to transmute it to. For example, sorrow into hope, fear into understanding, or aggravation into acceptance.

EXERCISE THIRTY-NINE

Creating an Ambient Psychic Transmutation System

To create this, we are going to work with a living plant to be both a battery and a psychic blueprint for the energy to follow. Any of the plants I listed in the previous chapter would work well, but you can also add creeping philodendrons and any form of ficus on the list, assuming we are creating this for an indoor space.

You will also need a (guiding) mineral to direct the energy for the entire filtration system. Again, those I listed in the previous chapter would all be great options. Finally, you will want a handful of support stones or copper pieces to help move the energy through the entire system. Exactly how many is up to you, but I prefer to have one for every corner of the space being covered.

Perform a level one cleansing on all of your supplies and on yourself. Place the guiding mineral at the base of the plant and the plant in a central location. Place the support minerals in each corner of the space with any points facing the plant. Stand in front of the plant and perform the Lasers! exercise, directing the flow of Source energy into the guide stone. As you do this, program the stone by verbally instructing it, saying:

> *"By my divine authority, I speak this into being that all* (insert your bad vibe here) *vibrations are transmuted into* (insert your good vibe here) *vibrations by way of this stone. What was toxic is now made beneficial through the power of Source and the covenant of the mind, body, and spirit as they reign in all worlds."*

Next, visualize the light moving from your hands to the guide stone, then outward to each of the support minerals. See them glow with Source energy and say:

"By my divine authority, I speak this into being these stones will act as channels for the energy in this space, bringing it to the guide stone. They work together to transmute the energies of this place. What was toxic is now made beneficial through the power of Source and the covenant of the mind, body, and spirit as they reign in all worlds."

Finally, bring your attention to the plant, visualize connecting to the guide stone, absorbing the Source energy and pulling it up through its leaves, which distribute back into the environment like a fountain. Program the entire system by saying:

"By my divine authority, I speak this into being: this system is complete! All (insert your bad vibe here) *vibrations are transmuted into* (insert your good vibe here) *vibrations by way of this stone, its tributaries, and this plant that all work in tandem with the power of Source. What was toxic is now made beneficial through the power of Source and the covenant of the mind, body, and spirit as they reign in all worlds. So it is."*

Spend a few moments visualizing the entire system come alive, glowing with the energy of Source. Observe how energy is directed from the support minerals to the central stone, how it connects to the plant and together they strip it of its former intentions and programing, before sending it upward to the leaves. See the negative particles break down and transform as they move through the guide stone and observe how nothing can escape this process. When you feel the intended energy begin to manifest in the space, you can disconnect from Source and let the system run on its own.

Check in daily to see if everything is still in working order. If it isn't, you can repair by performing the exercise again.

METHOD THREE:
ELEMENTAL TRANSMUTATION

In part 3, we talked about elemental cleansing, which is the practice of tapping into elemental energy and using it to remove different types of vibration. Elemental energy can also be used to transmute energy from one form to another. Elemental transmutation differs from the other forms of transmutation in that it transmutes through evolution or in some cases, devolving the energy from one elemental state to another. Let me explain, as I understand that all sounded like sci-fi jargon.

This form of transmutation is rooted in the understanding of that process I mentioned earlier called *wuxing*. In Chinese philosophy, wuxing is a conceptual scheme or map that follows the path of cosmic cycles. By studying it, we understand that the elements are progressing through two cycles: one of creation and one of destruction. We also learn that we can work with these cycles moving forward or going backward. This concept doesn't really have a parallel in Western civilization, which is a shame because it has massive implications for how we work with energy. I think wuxing fills in the blanks on a lot of previously misunderstood phenomena, but that is a topic for another day.

By incorporating the principles of wuxing into our spiritual practice, we are better equipped to transmute unwanted vibrations. I want to point out that what I am proposing is essentially taking some of the concepts in feng shui and essentially turning them into a channeling practice. If you want to get proficient in working with elemental energy in your spiritual practice, especially as it relates to your environment, you should invest some time in learning more about the principles involved as a side quest.

EXERCISE FORTY
Elemental Transmutation

Picking up where we left off in chapter 6 with the elements, I had merged the Western and Chinese models together, which gave us seven distinct elements: earth, wood, air, water, metal, fire, and spirit (Source). In my example, the cycle begins with earth and ends with fire; the element of spirit is all pervasive and present as an animating force in each of the other elements. For our purposes, we have to think of Spirit as the force behind the progression from one stage in the cycle to the next. Meaning that as one element changes into the next, its energy must be influenced by the element of Spirit. We have been working with this elemental energy throughout this entire book since the very beginning, which puts you in an excellent position to become an active participant in the elemental cycle.

Through our psychic and spiritual connection (Spirit), we are able to manipulate elemental energy, causing it to progress to the following stage in its cycle. It is going to take some getting used to and, as I mentioned at the beginning, a lot of experimentation, but I have found this practice to be really exciting in my own work. Alright, lets discuss the finer details.

The idea is that by psychically stimulating a vibration with a specific elemental energy, we can coax it into early transformation. In theory, we are introducing an alternate vibration that forces the original to become unstable in a way that it naturally would over time if it were exposed to that element on the physical plane. In practice, it feels a lot more like playing a game of Jenga but intentionally trying to make the stack fall. We always want to introduce this new vibration at the most foundational part of the original frequency to create the most instability to make the reaction occur. The most foundational part of any vibration is the tiny bit of Spirit that animates it and connects it to the All.

Doing all this might sound tricky, but if you are able to connect and channel elemental energy as I described in chapter 6, then the procedure of elemental transmutation is actually quite simple. All energy can be expressed as one of the elements; the hardest part is identifying which elemental energy the bad vibe you want to transmute corresponds with and then which elemental energy you want it to transmute into.

As for discerning the elemental nature of the bad vibe you want to transmute, this is one of those areas that might take some trial and error. My go-to technique is to rely on the emotions attached to the vibration, much like we did when we were learning to channel elemental energy. Emotions are a strong guide for psychic experience, so lean in on what you feel and let your spiritual body lead the way. Once you know the emotion(s), look for the element that best corresponds with it/them and go from there. Instead of rehashing all of that information, just reference the elemental breakdown in chapter 6.

Figuring out what elemental energy you want that bad vibe to transmute into is a totally different matter altogether. My advice is to reverse engineer the previous process. Figure out what emotion you want the energy to convey and then decide which element best corresponds to it. The reason you choose the element is up to you, though I recommend bringing energy that is beneficial and healing, if only because it will support the clearing and protection work you are already doing. When in doubt, transmute it into Spirit energy and direct it into your security system.

The elements interact with each other in different ways, depending on how they are applied. One result might require a slow, deliberate application while another might demand a swift, aggressive one. I can only help you determine this to a certain extent because every situation is different. What I can do is explain with a handy flow chart how the elements influence each other at different intensities.

If the effect is one that encourages the initial elemental energy, we will want to stay away from it, as it will only feed the bad vibration rather than force it into metamorphosis. We only want to work with energies that destabilize the original bad vibe.

MILD TO MODERATE APPLICATION

Earth smolders fire (destabilizing effect), nourishes wood (encouraging effect), blocks/absorbs water (destabilizing effect, excellent for transmutation), repels air (no effect), propagates metal (encouraging effect).

Wood fuels fire (encouraging effect), depletes water (destabilizing effect), stabilizes earth (encouraging effect), bends to air (no effect), dulls for metal (mild destabilizing effect).

Air fuels fire (encouraging effect), is absorbed by water (destabilizing effect), is repelled by earth (no effect), passes through wood (no effect), and passes through metal (no effect).

Water controls fire (destabilizing effect), invigorates wood (stabilizing effect), muddies earth (destabilizing effect), evaporates in air (destabilizing effect), and rusts metal (destabilizing effect).

Fire refines earth (stabilizing effect), consumes wood
(destabilizing effect), consumes air (destabilizing effect),
is extinguished by water (no effect), and melts metal
(destabilizing effect).

Metal impoverishes earth (destabilizing effect), chops wood
(destabilizing effect), moves through air (no effect),
contains water (stabilizing effect), and melts when
exposed to fire (no effect).

Spirit can be either stabilizing or destabilizing, depending on
its programmed intention.

LARGER, MORE CONCENTRATED APPLICATION

When we expose the same vibration to a larger, more concentrated
burst of elemental energy, the results are quite different in some of
these areas.

Earth smolders fire (destabilizing effect), buries wood
(destabilizing effect), blocks/absorbs water (destabilizing
effect, excellent for transmutation), repels air (no effect),
dulls metal (destabilizing effect).

Wood fuels fire (encouraging effect), depletes water
(destabilizing effect), depletes earth (destabilizing effect),
breaks to air (strong destabilizing effect), chips metal
(moderate to severe destabilizing effect).

Air smolders fire (destabilizing effect), pushes water
(destabilizing effect), is repelled by earth (no effect),
breaks wood (strong destabilizing effect), and erodes
metal (moderate to severe destabilizing effect).

Water extinguishes fire (severe destabilizing effect), rots wood (severe destabilizing effect), erodes earth (strong destabilizing effect), evaporates in air (destabilizing effect), and rusts metal (moderate to severe destabilizing effect).

Fire creates earth (stabilizing effect), consumes wood (strong destabilizing effect), consumes air (strong destabilizing effect), evaporates water (mild destabilizing effect), and melts metal (strong destabilizing effect).

Metal destroys earth (strong destabilizing effect), flattens wood (strong destabilizing effect), moves through air (no effect), contains water (strong stabilizing effect), and melts when exposed to fire (no effect).

Performing an elemental transmutation is easy on paper but, again, takes a bit of practice and a healthy bit of experimentation before it can be applied reliably. The risks are that we might either accidentally invigorate the bad vibe by sending the wrong type of elemental energy to it, or that we might assume the process is complete before it actually is, which will leave a loose end through which the energy can reemerge. I strongly advise that you check in with the object or space that you performed the transmutation on a day or two after just to make sure the work is done. Additionally, this is the type of spiritual work that our spirit guides love to help out on, so make sure you check in with them to get advice and feedback. They may even have a new technique or two to show you along the way!

Procedurally, we begin by sorting out the details that we have been talking about up to this point. We identify the bad vibration and the elemental energy that corresponds to it, then determine which elemental energy to introduce so we can destabilize the vibration and force it to move in a specific direction. Ideally, this direction is one that will benefit the environment or even heal the damage that the bad vibe might have caused.

Next, after grounding and preparing ourselves, we approach the afflicted object or location. Take a moment to reach out with your psychic senses to identify the afflicting vibration and continue to focus on it until you sense the element of Spirit present inside. This might take a few seconds, don't worry just keep focusing, use your own connection to Spirit to help you find it.

Perform the Channeling the Elements exercise from chapter 6. Instead of directing the elemental energy as you would a laser, allow it to travel to the vibration via the connection you both share to Spirit in the way a tiny current of electricity might travel down a wire. Do this for a period of three steady breaths and then stop, releasing your connection to both the element and the vibration.

Wait a few minutes, then observe the response with your psychic senses. If the vibration begins to destabilize, plug back in to both and continue the process until you feel the total shift has occurred. If, however, you don't observe any change, your options are to apply a greater volume of elemental energy or to adjust the type of elemental energy.

To increase the volume of elemental energy to the bad vibe, perform the exercise as before but allow for two or three times the amount of energy to transfer as the first time. Again, wait and see what happens. You can keep increasing in this way, observing the response and adjusting, for as long as you wish. By doing this, you run the risk of stimulating it or even clearing it accidentally.

CONCLUSION AND JOURNALING

Spiritual transmutation is a field of study that takes a lot of time and patience but that can be helpful when battling bad vibes of just about any kind. In this chapter, I shared three forms of spiritual transmutation, each relying on their own methods and techniques, but all geared at transforming bad vibrations into usable energy that pushed us closer to our dreams. The first method is approachable and is a great jumping point for the advanced work that is found in the other two methods. Start there and then dip your toes into the others when you are ready.

For this last chapter, journal about a bad vibration that you would like to transmute. Come up with a plan of action for how you are going to make it happen using one of the methods discussed in this chapter.

CONCLUSION

There is nothing worse than encountering an experience where you feel powerless. This is especially difficult when you can't see the thing that is threatening you and when others don't understand because they don't see it either. I have devoted my life, in one way or another, to helping people in these circumstances find a way through. If I hadn't seen the effects of bad vibes and felt them for myself, I am not entirely sure I'd believe it either. But the truth is often far stranger than we could imagine.

I have approached writing this book as if you, the reader, were a client of mine but also as if you were a peer. The process and flow of the exercises are all in alignment with how I would go about dealing with a preternatural disturbance and are representative of the work that I do as a professional medium.

While I am aware that I have a knack for the psychic and spiritual and that it is easy for someone like me to say this, I hope you have seen that claiming your spiritual authority and fighting back is not as difficult as it might seem at first. So much of the struggle is in remembering that you are the one with the power and that your power is exactly what those bad vibes want. If you remember nothing else, let it be that when it comes to matters of the spiritual, it's your energy, which means it has to play by your rules.

BIBLIOGRAPHY AND
RECOMMENDED READING

I mentioned several times throughout this book that I had lots of recommendations for those who were interested in taking their studies on a particular topic further. Here I deliver on those promises and have organized the titles by subject to make them easier when referencing.

PSYCHIC DEVELOPMENT AND DIVINATION

Andrews, Ted. *Psychic Protection*. Dragonhawk, 1998.

Auerbach, Loyd. *Mind Over Matter: A Comprehensive Guide to Discovering Your Psychic Powers*. Llewellyn, 2017.

Auryn, Mat. *Psychic Witch: A Metaphysical Guide to Meditation, Magick & Manifestation*. Llewellyn, 2020.

Auryn, Mat. *The Psychic Art of Tarot: Opening Your Inner Eye for More Insightful Readings*. Llewellyn, 2024.

Barnum, Melanie. *The Book of Psychic Symbols: Interpreting Intuitive Messages*. Llewellyn, 2012.

Barnum, Melanie. *Psychic Abilities for Beginners: Awaken Your Intuitive Senses*. Llewellyn, 2014.

Bruce, Robert. *Astral Dynamics: A New Approach to Out-of-Body Experience*. Hampton Roads, 1999.

Bruce, Robert. *The Practical Psychic Self-Defense Handbook: A Survival Guide.* Hampton Roads, 2011.

Buckland, Raymond. *The Fortune-Telling Book: The Encyclopedia of Divination and Soothsaying.* Visible Ink Press, 2003.

Dominguez Jr., Ivo. *Keys to Perception: A Practical Guide to Psychic Development.* Red Wheel/Weiser, 2017.

Miro, Shaheen, and Theresa Reed. *Tarot for Troubled Times: Confront Your Shadow, Heal Your Self & Transform the World.* Red Wheel/Weiser, 2019.

Reed, Theresa. *Tarot: No Questions Asked: Mastering the Art of Intuitive Reading.* Red Wheel/Weiser, 2020.

PSYCHIC AND SPIRITUAL ENERGY

Altea, Rosemary. *The Eagle and the Rose: A Remarkable True Story.* Grand Central, 2008.

Altea, Rosemary. *You Own the Power: Stories and Exercises to Inspire and Unleash the Force Within.* HarperCollins, 2010.

Andrews, Ted. *How To Do Psychic Readings Through Touch.* Llewellyn, 2014.

Andrews, Ted. *How to Heal with Color.* Llewellyn, 2014.

Andrews, Ted. *How to See and Read the Aura.* Llewellyn, 2006.

Andrews, Ted. *The Healer's Manual: A Beginner's Guide to Energy Healing for Yourself and Others.* Llewellyn, 2012.

Auryn, Mat. *Mastering Magick: A Course in Spellcasting for the Psychic Witch*. Llewellyn, 2022.

Brown, Simon. *The Feng Shui Bible: The Definitive Guide to Improving Your Home, Health, Finances, and Life*. Godsfield, 2005.

Bruce, Robert. *Practical Psychic Self-Defense: Understanding and Surviving Unseen Influences*. Hampton Roads, 2002.

Dominguez Jr., Ivo. *The Four Elements of the Wise: Working with the Magickal Powers of Earth, Air, Water, Fire*. Red Wheel/Weiser, 2021.

Heaven, Ross. *Spirit in the City*. Transworld, 2002.

Heaven, Ross, and Simon Buxton. *Darkness Visible: Awakening Spiritual Light Through Darkness Meditation*. Inner Traditions/Bear, 2005.

Pearson, Nicholas. *Foundations of Reiki Ryoho: A Manual of Shoden and Okuden*. Inner Traditions/Bear, 2018.

Penczak, Christopher. *The Mystic Foundation: Understanding and Exploring the Magical Universe*. Llewellyn, 2006.

RavenWolf, Silver. *MindLight: Secrets of Energy, Magick, and Manifestation*. Llewellyn, 2006.

Too, Lillian. *Feng Shui (Illustrated Encyclopedia)*. HarperCollins, 2013.

Too, Lillian. *Lillian Too's Essential Feng Shui: A Step-by-Step Guide to Enhancing Your Relationships, Health, and Prosperity.* Rider, 1998.

PRETERNATURAL STUDIES AND SPIRITS

Andrews, Ted. *How to Meet and Work with Spirit Guides.* Llewellyn, 2011.

Auerbach, Loyd. *A Paranormal Casebook: Ghost Hunting in the New Millennium.* Atriad Press, 2005.

Auerbach, Loyd. *ESP, Hauntings, and Poltergeists: A Parapsychologist's Handbook.* CreateSpace Independent Publishing Platform, 2016.

Auerbach, Loyd. *Hauntings and Poltergeists: A Ghost Hunter's Guide.* Ronin, 2005.

Auerbach, Loyd. *Mind Over Matter: A Comprehensive Guide to Discovering Your Psychic Powers.* Llewellyn, 2017.

Belanger, Michelle. *The Dictionary of Demons: Names of the Damned.* Llewellyn, 2010.

Belanger, Michelle. *The Ghost Hunter's Survival Guide: Protection Techniques for Encounters with the Paranormal.* Llewellyn, 2010.

Belanger, Michelle. *Haunting Experiences: Encounters with the Otherworldly.* Llewellyn, 2011.

Belanger, Michelle. *Walking the Twilight Path: A Gothic Book of the Dead.* Llewellyn, 2008.

Buckland, Raymond. *The Spirit Book: The Encyclopedia of Clairvoyance, Channeling, and Spirit Communication.* Visible Ink Press, 2005.

Dominguez Jr., Ivo. *Spirit Speak: Knowing and Understanding Spirit Guides, Ancestors, Ghosts, Angels, and the Divine.* Red Wheel/Weiser, 2008.

Miller, Jason. *Consorting with Spirits: Your Guide to Working with Invisible Allies.* Red Wheel/Weiser, 2022.

Penczak, Christopher. *Spirit Allies: Meet Your Team from the Other Side.* Weiser Books, 2002.

Welch, Michelle. *Spirits Unveiled: A Fresh Perspective on Angels, Guides, Ghosts & More.* Llewellyn, 2022.

PERSONAL SPIRITUAL DEVELOPMENT AND HEALING

Andrews, Ted. *How to Uncover Your Past Lives.* Llewellyn, 1992.

Barnum, Melanie. *Real Life Intuition: Extraordinary Stories from People Who Listen to Their Inner Voice.* Llewellyn, 2024.

Edward, John. *Crossing Over: The Stories Behind the Stories.* Sterling Ethos, 2010.

Edward, John. *One Last Time: A Psychic Medium Speaks to Those We Have Loved and Lost.* Penguin, 1999.

Pearson, Nicholas. *Crystals for Karmic Healing: Transform Your Future by Releasing Your Past.* Destiny Books, 2017.

Ruiz, Don Miguel, and Janet Mills. *The Four Agreements.* Amber-Allen, 2010.

Ruiz, Don Miguel, and Janet Mills. *The Mastery of Love.* Amber-Allen, 2010.

OTHER

Gawain, Shakti. *Creative Visualization: Use the Power of Your Imagination to Create What You Want in Your Life.* New World Library, 2002.

Pearson, Nicholas. *Crystal Basics Pocket Encyclopedia: The Energetic, Healing, and Spiritual Power of 450 Gemstones.* Inner Traditions/Bear, 2023.

Searle, John. "Minds, Brains, and Programs." 1980. *Behavioral and Brain Sciences* 3 (3): 417–424.

INDEX

Aliens, 124

Air (element), xiii, xv, xvi, 1, 2, 4, 8, 9, 12, 15, 16, 18–23, 25–38, 41, 50–52, 56, 70, 84–87, 90–93, 97, 98, 100–105, 108–113, 116–121, 127, 128, 133–146, 149–151, 154–161, 163–179, 181, 186–189, 195–197, 199, 201, 202, 205–209, 211–214, 217–221, 223–237, 240, 241

Anchors, 50, 60, 89–91, 96, 105, 199, 203, 214

Anchors (permanent), 89, 90

Anchors (temporary), 89

Anxiety, 4, 30, 50, 52, 82, 137, 156, 169, 181

Aspecting, 23, 24, 33

Attachments, xiv, 23, 24, 52, 56, 57, 113, 115, 117, 120, 128, 129, 137, 138, 142, 149, 161, 163, 165, 177–181, 186, 189, 190, 208, 216

Arcana, 50, 52

Body, 7, 8, 12, 19, 25–31, 33, 36, 43–45, 48, 54, 58, 71, 72, 76, 90, 92, 103, 104, 110, 114, 119, 127, 128, 131, 134, 136, 137, 141, 142, 144–146, 154, 155, 157, 164, 165, 172, 173, 175, 178, 179, 187, 189, 198, 200, 201, 205–208, 221, 225–228, 231

Centering, 29–31, 207

Channeling, 25, 33, 34, 37, 133, 139, 173, 187, 205, 226, 229, 235, 243

Chi traps, 109

Cleansing bath, 8, 93, 128, 143–146, 150, 161, 165, 166, 173, 180, 216

Collective consciousness, 97, 109, 123

Conscious psychic energy, 178

Cord cutting, 92, 161

Core beliefs, 7, 26, 27, 32–34, 39, 145, 156, 166, 205–208, 212, 220, 221

Crossing over, 188, 243

Curses, 20, 51, 94, 98, 100–102, 105, 110, 142, 165, 166

Curses (generational), 51, 101, 102

Demon, 20, 25, 49, 81, 82, 104, 113–115, 120, 124, 125, 128, 178, 182, 185, 198, 226, 242

Depression, 23, 44, 50, 52, 71–73, 82, 83, 129, 137, 169, 181

Divine authority, 25, 31, 51, 188, 227, 228

Earth (element), xiii, xv, xvi, 1, 2, 4, 8, 9, 12, 15, 16, 18–23, 25–38, 41, 50–52, 56, 70, 84–87, 90–93, 97, 98, 100–105, 108–113, 116–121, 127, 128, 133–146, 149–151, 154–161, 163–179, 181, 186–189, 195–197, 199, 201, 202, 205–209, 211–214, 217–221, 223–237, 240, 241

Egregore, 121, 123

Elemental, 112, 116–118, 121, 125, 141, 151, 178, 229–235

Elemental cleansing, 229

Elemental transmutation, 229–231, 234

Energy, xiii, xvi, 1, 2, 4, 8, 9, 12, 13, 15–20, 22, 23, 25–38, 41, 50–52, 56, 69, 70, 83–87, 90–93, 97, 98, 100–105, 108–113, 116–121, 127, 128, 132–146, 149–151, 155–161, 163–175, 177–181, 186–189, 195–197, 199, 201, 202, 204–209, 211–221, 223–237, 240, 241

Etheric cords, 91, 92, 133, 156, 161, 180

Etheric wildlife, 60, 117, 118, 163

Evil eye, 98–100, 105, 137

Exorcism, 70, 123, 128, 181, 182, 185, 186

Extraterrestrial, 112

Eviction, 182, 185–187, 189

Faeries, 116, 117

Feng shui, 109, 135, 229, 241, 242

Fire (element), xiii, xv, xvi, 1, 2, 4, 8, 9, 12, 15, 16, 18–23, 25–38, 41, 50–52, 56, 70, 84–87, 90–93, 97, 98, 100–105, 108–113, 116–121, 127, 128, 133–146, 149–151, 154–161, 163–179, 181, 186–189, 195–197, 199, 201, 202, 205–209, 211–214, 217–221, 223–237, 240, 241

Fumigation, 108, 143, 157

Ghost, 3, 4, 20, 70, 81, 83, 116–120, 122, 125, 177–179, 185, 242, 243

Grounding, 29–31, 136, 142, 146, 158, 165, 171, 173, 180, 207, 219, 235

Groups, 5, 96–98, 102, 103, 115, 117, 145, 169, 178

Grooming, 114

Gurus, 96

Haunting, xiv, xv, xvii, 42, 112, 117–120, 136, 149, 167, 169, 177, 179, 181, 189–191, 242

Haunted objects, 120

Home, xiv, 9, 11, 36, 51, 52, 83, 108, 110, 111, 119, 125, 127, 142, 144, 148, 169, 170, 178, 194, 199, 209, 211, 214, 215, 218, 219, 226, 241

Imprinting, 167–169, 179, 180

Incubi, 115, 116

Inner temple, 203, 205, 210–212, 219, 220

Iron, 123, 141, 142, 165, 168, 171, 172, 174, 175, 218

Higher Self, 28, 29, 31, 32, 184, 185, 187, 206

Land, 51, 52, 72, 107, 110, 120, 121, 131, 170, 171

Land spirit, 51, 120, 121

Ley lines, 20, 110, 111, 166, 172, 173, 226

Metal (element), xiii, xv, xvi, 1, 2, 4, 8, 9, 12, 15, 16, 18–23, 25–38, 41, 50–52, 56, 70, 84–87, 90–93, 97, 98, 100–105, 108–113, 116–121, 127, 128, 133–146, 149–151, 154–161, 163–179, 181, 186–189, 195–197, 199, 201, 202, 205–209, 211–214, 217–221, 223–237, 240, 241

Mild disturbance, 156

Mind (aspect of self), 7, 26, 27, 43, 48, 58, 71, 72, 76, 114, 119, 145, 154, 175, 178, 179, 198, 201, 206–208, 221, 225, 227, 228

Mind palace, 203, 209

Overshadowing, 23, 24, 33, 50–52, 114

Panic room, 203, 204, 219

Past lives, 51, 73–75, 86, 95, 124, 243

Pendulum, 42, 47, 48, 62

Personal security system, 197, 220

Poltergeist, 50, 52, 82–86, 111, 117, 119, 136, 163, 177, 179, 190, 242

Psychic cleansing, 104, 123, 131, 149

Psychic waste, 108, 109

Preternatural, 2, 11, 18, 20, 67, 105, 107, 112, 113, 121, 155, 167, 169, 177, 211, 237, 242

Reiki, 25, 134, 241

Residual haunting, 118, 120, 167, 169

Residual ghosts/spirits, 1–4, 7, 8, 11–13, 15, 17–27, 29, 31–36, 38, 39, 41, 43, 45, 48–52, 54–62, 65, 67, 69–72, 74–76, 80–82, 85–87, 90, 91, 93–96, 99–102, 105, 107–125, 127, 128, 131–139, 141–151, 153–156, 160–163, 165, 167, 169, 171, 172, 174–191, 194–204, 206, 208–214, 217–231, 233–237, 240–244

Residual psychic impressions, 117, 138, 168

Rude energy, 98, 105, 109, 156

Salt, 8, 93, 144–146, 165, 166, 168, 175, 180, 216

Security system, 186, 197, 200–204, 209, 218, 220, 222, 224, 226, 231

Sentient psychic energy, 179

Scale of Cleansing, 67, 129, 153, 175, 177, 190

Scanning, 41–44, 46–49, 55, 56, 153, 163, 173, 225

School, 97, 109, 125, 131, 136, 155, 166, 217

Shadow self, 76, 77, 79

Shadow work, 57, 75–78, 80, 86, 180, 186, 202

Sonic cleansing, 37, 85, 127, 128, 133, 136, 142, 144, 146–148, 153, 160, 170, 177, 231, 235

Source energy, 33, 38, 104, 134, 140, 164, 173, 187, 188, 205–207, 219–221, 226–228

Spirit (element), xiii, xv, xvi, 1, 2, 4, 8, 9, 12, 15, 16, 18–23, 25–38, 41, 50–52, 56, 70, 84–87, 90–93, 97, 98, 100–105, 108–113, 116–121, 127, 128, 133–146, 149–151, 154–161, 163–179, 181, 186–189, 195–197, 199, 201, 202, 205–209, 211–214, 217–221, 223–237, 240, 241

Spirit (entity), 2, 3, 8, 23, 24, 29, 34, 39, 41, 48, 49, 51, 52, 54–62, 71, 72, 75, 80–82, 85, 103, 109, 113–115, 118–120, 122, 123, 128, 129, 132, 133, 135, 137, 138, 142–146, 149, 157, 161–163, 165–167, 172, 173, 178–191, 198, 201, 204, 210–213, 216, 218, 220, 222, 224–226, 230–235, 241–243

Spirit (aspect of self), 7, 26, 43, 54, 71, 72, 76, 114, 119, 142, 154, 175, 179, 198, 201, 206, 221, 225, 227, 228

Spirit guides, 34, 39, 41, 55–58, 60–62, 80, 113, 114, 123, 128, 191, 204, 210, 211, 213, 220, 234, 242, 243

Succubi, 115

Tarot, 42, 47, 49, 54, 62, 183, 184, 239, 240

Thoughtform, 121–123, 211–213

Traditional hauntings, 119

Traditional ghosts, 3, 4, 20, 70, 81, 83, 116–120, 122, 125, 177–179, 185, 242, 243

Transmutation, 51, 110, 154, 155, 193,
210, 223–227, 229–234, 236

Trauma, 71–73, 83, 86, 102, 115, 129

Tributary, 111, 172–174, 228

Tuning fork, 146, 147

Twin flame, 94, 95

Vampire (psychic/emotional), 102–104, 208

Vibrations, xvi, 1, 2, 7, 11, 13, 15–17, 19–27, 37, 38,
41, 42, 44, 55, 61, 62, 65–67, 69, 71, 76, 78, 80, 81,
87, 89, 93, 97–99, 105, 107, 108, 110, 123, 125,
136, 137, 142–149, 153–156, 162, 163, 177, 188,
189, 196–198, 206, 207, 221, 224, 226–236

Visitor, 123, 124

Vital energy, 19, 85, 102, 181

Vortex, 111, 112, 125, 174, 175

Water (element), xiii, xv, xvi, 1, 2, 4, 8, 9, 12, 15, 16, 18–23,
25–38, 41, 50–52, 56, 70, 84–87, 90–93, 97, 98, 100–105,
108–113, 116–121, 127, 128, 133–146, 149–151,
154–161, 163–179, 181, 186–189, 195–197, 199, 201,
202, 205–209, 211–214, 217–221, 223–237, 240, 241

Willpower, 20, 50, 115, 182, 198, 199

Wood (element), xiii, xv, xvi, 1, 2, 4, 8, 9, 12, 15, 16, 18–23,
25–38, 41, 50–52, 56, 70, 84–87, 90–93, 97, 98, 100–105,
108–113, 116–121, 127, 128, 133–146, 149–151,
154–161, 163–179, 181, 186–189, 195–197, 199, 201,
202, 205–209, 211–214, 217–221, 223–237, 240, 241

Work, 2, 4, 9, 18, 20, 21, 23, 25, 28, 34, 41–44, 47, 49, 54–57, 61, 66, 69, 70, 73, 75–81, 83–86, 92, 93, 96, 97, 103, 104, 107, 109, 122, 125, 129, 132–134, 136–138, 141, 143, 145, 147–150, 154, 159, 160, 162, 167–172, 180–183, 186, 187, 189, 190, 196, 197, 200–202, 204, 205, 209, 211, 214, 216, 217, 219–223, 225–232, 234, 236, 237, 242

Wuxing, 135, 229

TO WRITE TO THE AUTHOR

If you wish to contact the author or would like more information about this book, please write to the author in care of Llewellyn Worldwide Ltd. and we will forward your request. Both the author and publisher appreciate hearing from you and learning of your enjoyment of this book and how it has helped you. Llewellyn Worldwide Ltd. cannot guarantee that every letter written to the author can be answered, but all will be forwarded. Please write to:

Devin Hunter
℅ Llewellyn Worldwide
2143 Wooddale Drive
Woodbury, MN 55125-2989

Please enclose a self-addressed stamped envelope for reply,
or $1.00 to cover costs. If outside the U.S.A., enclose
an international postal reply coupon.

Many of Llewellyn's authors have websites with additional information
and resources. For more information, please visit our website at
HTTP://WWW.LLEWELLYN.COM